19.95

Mahalia Jackson

AMERICAN WOMEN of ACHIEVEMENT

Mahalia Jackson

CHARLES K. WOLFE

CHELSEA HOUSE PUBLISHERS

NEW YORK · PHILADELPHIA

Chelsea House Publishers
EDITOR-IN-CHIEF   Nancy Toff
EXECUTIVE EDITOR   Remmel T. Nunn
MANAGING EDITOR   Karyn Gullen Browne
COPY CHIEF   Juliann Barbato
PICTURE EDITOR   Adrian G. Allen
ART DIRECTOR   Maria Epes
MANUFACTURING MANAGER   Gerald Levine

American Women of Achievement
SENIOR EDITOR   Richard Rennert

Staff for MAHALIA JACKSON
TEXT EDITOR   Jeff Klein
DEPUTY COPY CHIEF   Mark Rifkin
EDITORIAL ASSISTANT   Nicole Claro
PICTURE RESEARCHER   Patricia Burns
ASSISTANT ART DIRECTOR   Loraine Machlin
DESIGNER   Debora Smith
PRODUCTION MANAGER   Joseph Romano
PRODUCTION COORDINATOR   Marie Claire Cebrián
COVER ILLUSTRATOR   Gil Ashby

7   9   8   6

Library of Congress Cataloging-in-Publication Data

Wolfe, Charles K.

Mahalia Jackson / by Charles Wolfe.
p.   cm.—(American women of achievement)
Includes bibliographical references.
Summary: A biography of the renowned gospel singer who
hoped, through her art, to break down some of the barriers between black and white people.
ISBN 1-55546-661-3
    0-7910-0440-6 (pbk.)
1. Jackson, Mahalia, 1911–1972—Juvenile literature.   2. Gospel
musicians—United States—Biography—Juvenile literature.
[1. Jackson, Mahalia, 1911–1972.   2. Singers.   3. Afro-
Americans—Biography.]   I. Title.   II. Series.
ML3930.J2W64   1990
782.25′092—dc20   89-13903
[B]   CIP
[92]   AC MN

CONTENTS

AMERICAN WOMEN OF ACHIEVEMENT

Abigail Adams
women's rights advocate

Jane Addams
social worker

Louisa May Alcott
author

Marian Anderson
singer

Susan B. Anthony
woman suffragist

Ethel Barrymore
actress

Clara Barton
*founder of the American
Red Cross*

Elizabeth Blackwell
physician

Nellie Bly
journalist

Margaret Bourke-White
photographer

Pearl Buck
author

Rachel Carson
biologist and author

Mary Cassatt
artist

Agnes de Mille
choreographer

Emily Dickinson
poet

Isadora Duncan
dancer

Amelia Earhart
aviator

Mary Baker Eddy
*founder of the Christian
Science church*

Betty Friedan
feminist

Althea Gibson
tennis champion

Emma Goldman
political activist

Helen Hayes
actress

Lillian Hellman
playwright

Katharine Hepburn
actress

Karen Horney
psychoanalyst

Anne Hutchinson
religious leader

Mahalia Jackson
gospel singer

Helen Keller
humanitarian

Jeane Kirkpatrick
diplomat

Emma Lazarus
poet

Clare Boothe Luce
author and diplomat

Barbara McClintock
biologist

Margaret Mead
anthropologist

Edna St. Vincent Millay
poet

Julia Morgan
architect

Grandma Moses
painter

Louise Nevelson
sculptor

Sandra Day O'Connor
Supreme Court justice

Georgia O'Keeffe
painter

Eleanor Roosevelt
diplomat and humanitarian

Wilma Rudolph
champion athlete

Florence Sabin
medical researcher

Beverly Sills
opera singer

Gertrude Stein
author

Gloria Steinem
feminist

Harriet Beecher Stowe
author and abolitionist

Mae West
entertainer

Edith Wharton
author

Phillis Wheatley
poet

Babe Didrikson Zaharias
champion athlete

CHELSEA HOUSE PUBLISHERS

"REMEMBER THE LADIES"

MATINA S. HORNER

Remember the Ladies." That is what Abigail Adams wrote to her husband, John, then a delegate to the Continental Congress, as the Founding Fathers met in Philadelphia to form a new nation in March of 1776. "Be more generous and favorable to them than your ancestors. Do not put such unlimited power in the hands of the Husbands. If particular care and attention is not paid to the Ladies," Abigail Adams warned, "we are determined to foment a Rebellion, and will not hold ourselves bound by any Laws in which we have no voice, or Representation."

The words of Abigail Adams, one of the earliest American advocates of women's rights, were prophetic. Because when we have not "remembered the ladies," they have, by their words and deeds, reminded us so forcefully of the omission that we cannot fail to remember them. For the history of American women is as interesting and varied as the history of our nation as a whole. American women have played an integral part in founding, settling, and building our country. Some we remember as remarkable women who—against great odds—achieved distinction in the public arena: Anne Hutchinson, who in the 17th century became a charismatic religious leader; Phillis Wheatley, an 18th-century black slave who became a poet; Susan B. Anthony, whose name is synonymous with the 19th-century women's rights movement and who led the struggle to enfranchise women; and, in our own century, Amelia Earhart, the first woman to cross the Atlantic Ocean by air.

These extraordinary women certainly merit our admiration, but other women, "common women," many of them all but forgotten, should also be recognized for their contributions to American thought and culture. Women have been community builders; they have founded schools and formed voluntary associations to help those in need; they have assumed the major responsibility for rearing children, passing on from one generation to the next the values that keep a culture alive. These and innumerable other contributions, once ignored, are now being recognized by scholars, students, and the public. It is exciting and gratifying to realize that a part of our history that was hardly acknowledged a few generations ago is now being studied and brought to light.

In recent decades, the field of women's history has grown from obscurity to a politically controversial splinter movement to academic respectability, in many cases mainstreamed into such traditional disciplines as history, economics, and psychology. Scholars of women, both female and male, have organized research centers at such prestigious institutions as Wellesley College, Stanford University, and the University of California. Other notable centers for women's studies are the Center for the American Woman and Politics at the Eagleton Institute of Politics at Rutgers University; the Henry A. Murray Research Center for the Study of Lives, at Radcliffe College; and the Women's Research and Education Institute, the research arm of the Congressional Caucus on Women's Issues. Other scholars and public figures have established archives and libraries, such as the Schlesinger Library on the History of Women in America, at Radcliffe College, and the Sophia Smith Collection, at Smith College, to collect and preserve the written and tangible legacies of women.

From the initial donation of the Women's Rights Collection in 1943, the Schlesinger Library grew to encompass vast collections documenting the manifold accomplishments of American women. Simultaneously, the women's movement in general and the academic discipline of women's studies in particular also began with a narrow definition and gradually expanded their mandate. Early causes such as woman suffrage and social reform, abolition and organized labor were joined by newer concerns such as the history of women in business and the professions and in politics and government; the study of the family; and social issues such as health policy and education.

Women, as historian Arthur M. Schlesinger, jr., once pointed out, "have constituted the most spectacular casualty of traditional history.

They have made up at least half the human race, but you could never tell that by looking at the books historians write." The new breed of historians is remedying that omission. They have written books about immigrant women and about working-class women who struggled for survival in cities and about black women who met the challenges of life in rural areas. They are telling the stories of women who, despite the barriers of tradition and economics, became lawyers and doctors and public figures.

The women's studies movement has also led scholars to question traditional interpretations of their respective disciplines. For example, the study of war has traditionally been an exercise in military and political analysis, an examination of strategies planned and executed by men. But scholars of women's history have pointed out that wars have also been periods of tremendous change and even opportunity for women, because the very absence of men on the home front enabled them to expand their educational, economic, and professional activities and to assume leadership in their homes.

The early scholars of women's history showed a unique brand of courage in choosing to investigate new subjects and take new approaches to old ones. Often, like their subjects, they endured criticism and even ostracism by their academic colleagues. But their efforts have unquestionably been worthwhile, because with the publication of each new study and book another piece of the historical patchwork is sewn into place, revealing an increasingly comprehensive picture of the role of women in our rich and varied history.

Such books on groups of women are essential, but books that focus on the lives of individuals are equally indispensable. Biographies can be inspirational, offering their readers the example of people with vision who have looked outside themselves for their goals and have often struggled against great obstacles to achieve them. Marian Anderson, for instance, had to overcome racial bigotry in order to perfect her art and perform as a concert singer. Isadora Duncan defied the rules of classical dance to find true artistic freedom. Jane Addams had to break down society's notions of the proper role for women in order to create new social institutions, notably the settlement house. All of these women had to come to terms both with themselves and with the world in which they lived. Only then could they move ahead as pioneers in their chosen callings.

Biography can inspire not only by adulation but also by realism. It helps us to see not only the qualities in others that we hope to emulate but also, perhaps, the weaknesses that made them "human." By helping us identify with the subject on a more personal level they help us to feel that we, too, can achieve such goals. We read about Eleanor Roosevelt, for example, who occupied a unique and seemingly enviable position as the wife of the president. Yet we can sympathize with her inner dilemma: an inherently shy woman who had to force herself to live a most public life in order to use her position to benefit others. We may not be able to imagine ourselves having the immense poetic talent of Emily Dickinson, but from her story we can understand the challenges faced by a creative woman who was expected to fulfill many family responsibilities. And though few of us will ever reach the level of athletic accomplishment displayed by Wilma Rudolph or Babe Zaharias, we can still appreciate their spirit, their overwhelming will to excel.

A biography is a multifaceted lens. It is first of all a magnification, the intimate examination of one particular life. But at the same time, it is a wide-angle lens, informing us about the world in which the subject lived. We come away from reading about one life knowing more about the social, political, and economic fabric of the time. It is for this reason, perhaps, that the great New England essayist Ralph Waldo Emerson wrote, in 1841, "There is properly no history: only biography." And it is also why biography, and particularly women's biography, will continue to fascinate writers and readers alike.

Mahalia Jackson

Mahalia Jackson, gospel's top recording star, in 1954, the year her weekly radio program debuted on the CBS radio network.

ONE

"We're on CBS!"

By 7:30 in the evening on September 24, 1954, a crowd began to gather outside the doors to the studio theater in the huge Wrigley Building in downtown Chicago. Diners coming out of the plush Wrigley restaurant just across the hallway wondered what was going on. What kind of event could cause so much excitement on a hot Friday night?

At 8:00 P.M., the doors to the theater finally opened, and hordes of people rushed in, quickly filling the 400 available seats. Within 30 minutes, the house was jammed, and the ushers were locking the doors to prevent any unwanted interruptions. A new CBS network radio program, simply entitled "The Mahalia Jackson Show," was about to begin taping in a little more than an hour.

In the glassed-in control room overlooking the small stage, engineers checked their microphones and anxiously watched their meters to make sure the sound levels were right. They knew that the tape would not air on the nationwide radio network until Sunday night at 10:05. Nevertheless, they wanted to get things right the first time through, to preserve the feel of a live radio show performed before a live studio audience. It was a type of show that had seldom been played on network radio before. The program featured gospel, a form of music that was part jazz, part hymn, and part spiritual—and yet it was not quite like any of them.

There was no big orchestra on stage, just a piano and an electric organ, placed at right angles to each other so they formed an inverted V. Between them was a large rectangular microphone about the size of a shoe box. It rested on a floor stand and was topped with a metal crown bearing the initials *CBS*.

Sitting at the piano was a small, intense young woman with a short, stylish hairdo and a heavy gold bracelet on each wrist; her name was Mildred Falls, and she had been Mahalia Jackson's piano player for seven years. She was extremely familiar with Jackson's repertoire and vocal style, but more important, she knew what to do when the spirit got hold of Mahalia: She would improvise, expanding on the melody like a jazz musician. Over at the electric organ, with its two keyboards and rows of switches, was a thin young man with a gentle face and tiny mustache; he was Ralph Jones, a newcomer fresh from a job at a little storefront church on South State Street in Chicago. Across the stage from them was a white vocal quartet organized by the veteran Chicago singer and music arranger Jack Halloran, the man in charge of the overall musical direction of the show.

This small group had been rehearsing for a week, astonishing the CBS engineers with the vitality and excitement it generated. But the engineers were also worried about the upcoming performance: Jackson seldom sang a song the same way twice. It sounded as though the 41-year-old singer and her 2 accompanists followed the music wherever it took them, and that made each rendition of a particular song different every time they performed it. On one occasion, Jackson had performed a slow, moody piece called ''I Believe'' in 2 minutes and 40 seconds; the second time she rehearsed the song, it lasted 3 minutes and 20 seconds. In the clockwork world of network radio, an unscheduled discrepancy of 40 seconds could ruin a show's intricate schedule —and cause CBS to fail to air 2 lucrative commercials.

Eventually, the cause of all this concern stepped to the microphone. Mahalia Jackson was a big, heavyset woman with a warm, easy smile that contrasted sharply with the intensity of her eyes. Her hair was swept back in the sort of tight bun popular that year, and her large golden earrings flashed in the spotlights.

Jackson looked around, as nervous and concerned as any young star about to make a debut on one of the country's largest radio networks would be. Yet she was no newcomer to performing before large audiences. Mahalia Jackson—known to her friends and relatives as Halie—was, according to her record company press agents, the ''queen of gospel singers.'' She had already presented four concerts at New York's famed Carnegie Hall, headlined numerous gospel singing tours, completed a string of appearances in Europe, appeared on Ed Sullivan's nationwide television show, and attracted more than 50,000 people to Mahalia Jackson Day in Dayton, Ohio. Hers was a household name to millions of black Americans, and though millions of

Jackson with her longtime accompanist, Mildred Falls. Expert at improvisation, Falls was one of the best pianists in gospel.

white Americans had by now heard of her, few of them knew anything about the vast, complex world of gospel music.

Jackson looked over the audience at her first radio show and saw that most of the faces before her were white, with only small groups of blacks clustered here and there throughout the auditorium. To win their approval would be a real test for her music.

As Mildred Falls began to run through some chords on her piano, Jack Halloran came over to Jackson with the musical score for "I Believe." The arranger suggested that she begin singing

15

on the eighth bar of the song. "Jack," the vocalist replied, "don't talk to me about bars. What *word* do you want me to start on?"

After that question was settled, the performers began a run-through of their first number. The band kicked off with a rocking introduction, and Jackson started singing. Suddenly, she broke off, motioning to her musicians to stop. It wasn't right. The audience was just sitting there, staring politely, like so many cardboard cutouts. The singer decided that perhaps some instructions to her white listeners were in order. "You got to learn how to clap, babies," she told them. "You got to help Mahalia, or Mahalia's scared she's going to fall right on her face. Now look"—and she proceeded to demonstrate how to clap along with the song.

Then Jackson addressed some words to the smaller contingent of black fans, most of whom needed little instruction

Jackson rehearsing for an appearance on "The Ed Sullivan Show," television's leading variety program, in 1960. Her appearances on the show, dating back to the 1950s, helped introduce gospel music to white America.

about how to respond to gospel music. "Now remember," she said, "you all not in church—though you ought to be. No jumping up and down, no stomping; that interferes with the sounds going out over the mikes. Now you know Mahalia can't have that. You've got to remember, we're not in church—we're on CBS!"

Five minutes later, announcer Hal Stark stepped up to the mike to say, in his rich, old-time radio voice, that "The Mahalia Jackson Show" was on the air. Taking a deep breath, Jackson began singing in a slow, bluesy style:

I sing because my soul is happy,
I sing because I'm free,
For His eye, it is on the little old spar-
  row,
And I know He is watching over you
  and me.

The song, entitled "His Eye Is on the Sparrow," was a gospel hymn written in 1905 by an Atlanta woman named Civilla Surfee. It became popular in black churches in the 1930s, and Jackson had decided to use it as her opening number. When she finished her abbreviated version of the song, waves of applause rolled through the small auditorium. The tension was broken for Jackson, who was getting her first taste of how the big-time music business worked. Both the blacks and whites in the audience also began to relax and let themselves get into the spirit of things. Now the show was ready to roll.

In 1954, many Americans still thought of gospel music as a poor second cousin to jazz or believed the phrase meant spirituals, like "Swing Low Sweet Chariot." Few of them knew much about the modern gospel music that had originated in Chicago in the 1930s, when composers such as Thomas A. Dorsey had drawn on the increasing popularity of solo singers (as opposed to church quartets and choirs) to establish a whole new style of black church music—a style based as much on the popular new sounds of the commercial music world as on traditional forms of church music. Occasionally, one of these gospel songs, such as Dorsey's "Peace in the Valley," managed to make it onto the "Hit Parade," a radio show featuring the nation's top tunes. But these gospel songs were few.

About 1950, however, songs with a religious message began to become popular. Old hymns such as "Whispering Hope" and "How Great Thou Art," as well as newer songs such as "This Old House" and "It Is No Secret, What God Can Do," suddenly appeared on the best-seller lists for sheet music, dressed up in slick, modern arrangements with formal choirs and big orchestras full of violins. One of the men most responsible for this trend was a Columbia Records producer named Mitch Miller. Always looking for new talent, he heard Jackson sing at several concerts and persuaded her to switch over to his record label in early 1954. With all the new interest in gospel music, he thought, she had a chance of appealing to a much wider audience and becoming a star.

Miller began to look for new songs for Jackson, alerting the big Columbia publicity department to get ready to

Columbia Records producer Mitch Miller with Jackson at a mid-1950s recording session. A pivotal figure in gospel's crossover into the mainstream, Miller signed Jackson onto his label in early 1954.

swing into action. Part of his plan for promoting Jackson involved radio. Miller contacted his friend Lou Cowan, who worked out of Chicago and produced a hit radio program called "Quiz Kids." The Columbia producer told Cowan of the big plans he had for Jackson and suggested that Cowan might want to audition her for a radio series. Cowan agreed.

On Monday, September 20, Cowan taped a sample of Jackson's singing and flew to New York. There he played the tape for CBS president William Paley, and that Friday he had a contract for "The Mahalia Jackson Show." The whole process had taken five days. "That's what you call the power of prayer," Jackson said later.

With the first song out of the way, Jackson began to perform the kind of songs for which she was known. One was "Joshua Fought the Battle of Jericho," an old spiritual that had been sung by slaves before the Civil War. Next came "Summertime," one of the pop songs she had just learned. Featuring a slow, haunting melody, it was from the Broadway musical *Porgy and Bess* and had been a favorite of jazz singers for years. In the middle of the song, Jackson found herself inserting a few lines from one of her favorite spirituals, "Sometimes I Feel Like a Motherless Child." The result was a powerful creation, a symbolic mixture of pop, jazz, and gospel that displayed the kind of versatility of which Jackson was capable. Then the tempo picked up again as the group rocked into one of its old favorites, the old spiritual "Didn't It Rain," about Noah and his ark. Jackson sang:

> Well, it rained forty days, forty nights
> without stopping,
> Noah looked up and the rain stopped
> dropping,
> Knock at the window, knock at the
> door,
> Calling, "Brother Noah, can you take
> one more?"

The piano and organ caught the spirit of the music, and Jackson began to sway back and forth with the beat. The sound engineers looked nervously at their meters, not used to having so much action in front of a microphone. The singer's voice, powerful enough to begin with, was now getting stronger as she moved into the second half of the song.

> Didn't it rain, children, all night long?
> Didn't it?
> Didn't it?
> Didn't it rain, all night long?

Each "Didn't it?" became louder and more infectious, with Jackson singing the words much like tenor saxophonists in rhythm-and-blues bands phrase their notes. Mildred Falls began to echo the singer's phrasing on her piano.

> Just listen to how it's raining,
> Just listen to how it's raining,
> Just listen to how it's raining,
> Some morning, some morning,
> Just listen to how it's raining.

By then, the audience needed no encouragement. It was shouting, clapping, dancing in place, urging the singer on. When the piece finally came to an end, the applause was so loud that the producers had to call an intermission to calm the listeners.

When order was restored, Jackson launched into "Trees," a rather mushy number that had been foisted on her by Halloran. She had doubts about the song but had learned it to appease her producers. Now, backed by Halloran's smooth, all-white vocal quartet, the song sounded pretty good, she admitted to herself.

Several more gospel numbers followed. When Jackson sang a verse of "His Eye Is on the Sparrow" to close out the show, the people in the audience stood on their feet and applauded. Producer John Lewellen came out of his control booth beaming. "You were a smash," he told the singer. "We've got us a show!"

Two nights later, Jackson sat in her Chicago apartment with a friend. They stared at the radio, waiting for the 10 o'clock news to end so she could hear what the show sounded like. She pursed her lips in concentration, thinking about how much was riding on the show, when she heard the opening strains of "His Eye Is on the Sparrow."

Jackson knew that only a handful of black singers in 1954 had their own network show that reached hundreds of stations across the country. She realized that in her own world of black gospel music, she had made it to the top. But now, with her new Columbia Records contract and the radio show, she was ready for a more difficult chal-

CBS founder and president William S. Paley, impressed by a tape of Jackson's audition, gave the immediate go-ahead to plans for "The Mahalia Jackson Show" on CBS Radio.

lenge: to win over white America to the sounds of black religious music.

In the upcoming years, Jackson would have to make some compromises to reach that goal. She would have to enlarge her repertoire to get people who favored Broadway show tunes and other types of songs to listen to her. Some would accuse her of selling out, of commercializing the Lord's music. Others would accuse her of turning her back on her black heritage.

As Jackson thought about what

would be expected of her, she realized with a start that it was Sunday night, and for one of the few Sunday nights in her life she was not in church. Were the compromises already beginning? she wondered.

Tormented by doubts, Jackson felt that the show seemed to go by in an instant. When it was over, she turned to her friend and muttered, "I could have been better."

The newspaper reviews the next morning, however, had no such reservations. "She's the greatest!" wrote the *Chicago Sun-Times*. "When Mahalia begins to sing, even the elevator men in the building begin to bounce," wrote the *Tribune*. Soon, the phones in Jackson's apartment were ringing with messages of congratulations and requests for interviews. Radio stations wanted Jackson to send them her records. National magazines wanted her to explain gospel to them. American music was getting ready to embrace Mahalia Jackson, its next big star.

A market scene in New Orleans at the turn of the century. Jackson was deeply influenced by New Orleans, her childhood home.

T W O

Pinching Town

In the months that followed her first radio appearance, Mahalia Jackson spent a fair amount of her time giving newspaper interviews. People were curious about where she came from and how she had learned to sing the way she did.

It all started down in Louisiana, Jackson would say, with her mother's family, the Clarks. In 1890, her uncle Porterfield Clark (Uncle Porter, Jackson usually called him) lived with his 10 brothers and sisters on a rice plantation in Pointe Coupée Parish. The plantation, nicknamed Gumstump by its workers, was near Baton Rouge, in the south-central part of the state, and had formerly been a slave plantation. After the Civil War ended in 1865, a number of black families remained on the plantation to work as sharecrop-pers, renting the land they farmed from its owners in exchange for a portion of the crops.

Porterfield Clark's parents—Mahalia Jackson's maternal grandparents—were among those who worked as sharecroppers on the plantation. His father, Paul, who did all the corn grinding for the plantation and was a well-known man in the community, spent many Sundays in the local church as a guest preacher. Porter's mother, Cecile, managed to raise most of her 11 children before she died at the relatively young age of 46. It was a hard life, even by the standards of those pioneer days. "My grandparents lived in a little log cabin," Mahalia Jackson wrote in her autobiography, *Movin' on Up*. "They cooked over a wood-burning fireplace. They chinked the floor cracks with rags and they took barrel hoops and decorated them with colored paper and bits of cloth for decorations for their home. . . . They lived and died in that same cabin."

Porterfield Clark, the oldest of Paul and Cecile's sons, was always fascinated by the big riverboats that steamed past the plantation on the Atchafalaya River on their way to New Orleans, which was 100 miles to the south. He eventually befriended some of the captains and learned how to cook on the tiny wood and coal galleys found on most of the boats. Before long, he became an accomplished cook and graduated to the bigger steamboats running on the nearby Mississippi.

By 1900, Clark had moved to New Orleans, where he married, and began working to get his brothers and sisters to join him. Using his connections with the steamboat companies, he was able to get them bargain rates, and one by one the Clarks left the old plantation and joined Porterfield in the modern, bustling city of New Orleans, which then had a population of 350,000 (the biggest town most of them had seen until then was New Roads, Louisiana,

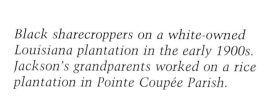

Black sharecroppers on a white-owned Louisiana plantation in the early 1900s. Jackson's grandparents worked on a rice plantation in Pointe Coupée Parish.

A Mississippi River steamboat on the New Orleans waterfront. Jackson's uncle, Porterfield Clark, a cook for a riverboat line, moved to New Orleans in 1900.

which had a population of 1,200). The move meant a big change for the Clarks, but it also meant a chance for a better life.

By 1912, all seven of the Clark sisters, along with five of their children, were living on Water Street in a four-room "shotgun" house—so called because all the rooms were lined up one behind another, supposedly enabling someone to stand at the front door, fire a shotgun, and see the shell go all the way through the house and out the back door. In front of the house were train tracks, then a levee with its bank built up to keep back the Mississippi, and then the river itself.

That spring, Charity Clark, the youngest of the seven sisters, discovered that she was pregnant. The father was Johnny Jackson, a slim, handsome man with deep-set eyes and a pencil-thin mustache, who worked on the wharf during the day and ran a barbershop in the evenings. Because he already had a family living in a nearby community and often spent his weekends there, he had no plans to marry Charity. Nor did Charity want to marry him, particularly because Louisiana law at the time made it hard for a "law-married" woman to buy anything substantial without her husband's signed consent.

Charity's time came on Saturday, October 26, 1912, prompting the Clark sisters to send for a local midwife named Granny Lee, who later that day assisted Charity in the birth of her baby girl. The child was born with infected eyes and bowed legs, but otherwise she was a lively, curious baby. Charity decided to name her after her sister, who was nicknamed Duke but whose real name was Mahala. Charity filled out the baby's name on the birth certificate as Mahala—the *i* would come later—and coupled it with Jackson, the father's surname.

In the early 1900s, a time when racial tensions were especially high in the South, there were worse places for a black to grow up than in New Orleans. The neighborhood where the Clarks lived was a bustling, colorful area centered around a street called Magazine—named after the French word *magasin*, meaning store. "It was a mixed-up neighborhood," Jackson wrote in her autobiography, "with Negroes, French, Creoles and Italians all trying to scratch out a living." Small grocery stores, trinket shops, and pushcarts lined the streets, and young Mahala darted among them, running errands, playing, visiting. On the other side of the street was the levee, which served as another playground. "We used to sit out there and sing songs with ukuleles," Jackson recalled, "and bake sweet potatoes in fires made from driftwood and catch all the fish and shrimp and crabs we wanted."

Mahala was Charity's second child; her brother, Peter, had been born three years earlier on the plantation in Pointe Coupée. He was quick to resent his scrawny little sister tagging along after him and started calling her "fishhooks" because of her bowed legs. Indeed, her bowleggedness was a problem. When her mother took Mahala to various doctors to examine her legs, their advice was to correct the problem by operating on them—a suggestion that Charity Clark rejected. Instead, she began her own treatment, massaging Mahala's legs every night. Before long, the Clark sisters claimed they could see real improvement in Mahala.

In June 1918, with no warning or illness whatsoever, Charity Clark died. She was just 30 years old. Her sisters took her body upriver to Gumstump, where it was laid to rest with other generations of Clarks.

On the trip back to New Orleans, the sisters discussed the plight of Charity's two children. Aunt Duke—the aunt for whom Mahala was named—settled the issue by saying, "I'll take 'em both." She was, after all, the one who really ran the Clark clan. Besides, Aunt Duke had already raised a child; her son, Fred, was almost grown and starting to work on the river docks. Upon Aunt Duke's return, five-year-old Mahala and eight-year-old Peter moved the six blocks from their late mother's house to their new home.

Aunt Duke was small, wiry, quick tempered, and sternly religious—the complete opposite from the warm, outgoing Charity. "She was a dark brown-skinned woman," Jackson later said of her aunt, "who carried herself very

Bessie Smith, one of the earliest blues stars. When Jackson was a child, the blues was one of several black musical genres popular in New Orleans.

straight and she had gray eyes that looked right through you."

But even with a strict, no-nonsense aunt like Duke Clark, it was impossible for young Jackson not to be swept up by the music that filled the city of New Orleans. Brass bands played at funerals, ragtime piano players entertained in clubs, and dance orchestras in high society played quadrilles, an old French dance that resembled a modern square dance. Along the river, dockworkers and steamboat hands sang work songs, and along Magazine vegetable vendors even hawked their wares with catchy singsong chants. Farther downtown, in a district called Storyville, men with colorful names, like pianist Ferdinand "Jelly Roll" Morton, trombonist Edward "Kid" Ory, and cornetist Joe "King" Oliver, mixed the music of the brass bands with the folk blues of rural blacks and created a new type of music people were beginning to call jazz.

Mahala learned her first song, a spiritual called "Oh Pal, Oh God," from an old man she met while she was playing on the levee. When she was four, she entertained some of her mother's acquaintances with a different type of song, the bawdy "Balling the Jack," which she had heard through the windows of neighborhood dance halls. On Sundays, though, she sang a different tune: She performed with the children's choir at the Plymouth Rock Baptist Church. In a voice that made her sound much bigger than she was, Mahala sang out such numbers as "Oh, Hand Me Down My Silver Trumpet, Gabriel."

Mahala clearly liked to sing. After she began attending school, teachers sometimes had to punish her because she hummed constantly while she went about her work. On those occasions, she would protest that she did not realize she was humming out loud.

In the strict religious household of Aunt Duke, Mahala did not dare repeat her performance of "Balling the Jack." Nevertheless, she learned about other styles of nonreligious music through her father, whom she often visited. Every now and then, her father's sister—a traveling vaudeville performer who, with her husband, appeared in an act called Camp and Camp and often worked traveling tent shows with Ma Rainey, one of the first of the great blues singers—stopped by the house. The husband-and-wife team liked to tell stories to Mahala about some of the legendary black singers of the day and about the exciting new music they sang. One day, after they heard Mahala's voice, they pleaded with her to join their act and travel with them. Aunt Duke would not allow it, though.

Duke's son, Fred, provided the young singer with another way to hear contemporary popular music: He owned a Victrola, a relatively new invention. Powered by a spring wound by a hand crank, this phonograph played big, brittle records at 78 revolutions per minute. Fred had a sizable collection of these records.

Only a few years earlier, in 1920, a large record company in New York called Okeh had released "Crazy Blues," cut by a stage singer named Mamie Smith. It was a big hit, but more important, it was the first blues song recorded by a black singer. Within four years of the record's release, blues vocalists such as Ma Rainey and Bessie Smith had made best-selling records that were being played all over the country.

Mahala found that her cousin Fred owned a big stack of these blue-labeled discs. "Aunt Duke never knew it," she wrote in her autobiography, "but when she was away . . . I played Fred's records

Ma Rainey, another early blues star, onstage with an unidentified actor in the 1920s. The individual recordings of Rainey and Bessie Smith, issued in the 1920s, deeply influenced young Jackson.

A New Orleans street in the early 1930s. Born in 1912 and orphaned in 1918, Mahalia Jackson (she didn't add the i to her first name until she was 22) was raised by a strict but loving aunt.

all day long—especially the blues songs of Bessie Smith. Bessie was my favorite, but I never let people know I listened to her. Mamie Smith, the other famous blues singer, had a prettier voice, but Bessie's had more soul in it. She dug right down and kept it in you. Her music haunted you even when she stopped singing."

One of the records Mahala especially liked was Bessie Smith's version of "St. Louis Blues," written by composer W. C. Handy. Its opening line, "I hate to see that evening sun go down," had a haunting effect on Mahala. So did Bessie Smith's rendition of "Careless

Love," with its long, drawn-out phrases and molasses-slow tempo. Years later, Jackson told *down beat* magazine: "I'd play that record over and over again, and Bessie's voice would come out so full and round. And I'd make my mouth do the same thing. And before you know, all the people would stand outside the door and listen." Indeed, jazz critics have often claimed that had Jackson chosen to sing the blues instead of gospel, she could have been the "next Bessie Smith" and one of the greatest blues singers ever. Although she eventually turned her back on the blues of Bessie Smith, Ma Rainey, and

Mamie Smith, she always retained some of their feeling and style in her music.

While Mahala was growing up in the 1920s, jazz became the dominant form of music in New Orleans. Although she was not allowed to go into the downtown clubs and dance halls where the great jazz pioneers were playing, she heard her share of the music at various lodge dances, fish fries, and even funerals. "When there was going to be a big fish fry or lodge dance," she wrote, "they would fill a wagon up with a load of hay or they'd put some chairs in it. The brass band—some of them were five pieces—would climb up in that wagon and they would drive around town, stopping and playing at every street corner to drum up a crowd."

The same bands also had a more serious function: They played for funerals. At the start of the service, the band would play slow, organlike hymns in front of the church and would then march behind the hearse all the way to the cemetery, playing pieces like "The Old Rugged Cross" or "Nearer My God to Thee." Upon returning from the cemetery after the funeral, the same band would jazz it up, playing tunes like "Didn't He Ramble." Along the sidewalk, friends and followers would form a "second line" to dance and celebrate—a joyous reaffirmation of life to follow the sad ritual of death. Young Jackson was fascinated with all this— and with how closely jazz and church music were mixed in such a tradition.

Jelly Roll Morton, one of the top pianists and composers in early jazz. Like many other jazz greats, he performed most often in New Orleans's Storyville area.

31

King Oliver's Creole Jazz Band in a 1924 publicity photo. Oliver, one of jazz's earliest stars, stands third from the left.

In spite of her interest in all these forms of music, Mahala confined her own singing to the church. By the time she was 14, she was becoming known as the skinny little girl with the big voice not only in her neighborhood, called Pinching Town (a play on the name of the well-to-do white section called Pension Town), but in other parts of New Orleans as well. In Pinching Town, with its dirt streets, barrooms, and small stores, people had to pinch pennies and scratch out a living by working as maids or cooks for rich white families. One of the neighbor-hood's leading churches was the Mount Moriah Mission Baptist Church, and it was there that Mahala joined the choir and first won respect as a singer.

Mahala liked the stately, formal mu-sic of the choir, but she delighted even more in the music of the congregation. "All around me I could hear the foot-tapping and hand-clapping," she wrote in her autobiography. And though she always remained a Baptist, Jackson be-came fascinated with a different type of church, the Sanctified Church, which was next door to her house. "Those people had no choir and no organ," she wrote. "They used the drum, the cym-bal, the tambourine, and the steel tri-angle. Everybody in there sang and they clapped and stomped their feet and sang with their whole bodies. They had a beat, a powerful beat . . . and their music was so strong and expressive it used to bring the tears to my eyes. I believe the blues and jazz and even the rock-and-roll stuff got their beat from the Sanctified Church."

While the Baptist churchgoers would sing stately old hymns such as "Amaz-ing Grace," the congregation in the Sanctified Church would tear into up-tempo shouters such as "I'm So Glad Jesus Lifted Me Up." Mahala loved them both, and by the time she was 15, she was already beginning to wonder how she could fit both types of music

The congregation of a New Orleans Baptist church in the 1920s. By the time she was a teenager, Jackson's choir singing had made her locally famous.

into her life. She also started to wonder how the blues of Bessie Smith and the jazz of the New Orleans lodge halls fit into the picture. It was all part of the complex black musical tradition that was just beginning to assert itself in America during the 1920s, and in some special way Mahala Jackson sensed she would play a part in it.

Part of the annual Mardi Gras carnival in New Orleans. Caught up in the city's freewheeling atmosphere, the young Jackson was kicked out of her aunt's house and on her own at age 15.

THREE

Going to Chicago

Shortly after she had finished the eighth grade, Mahala Jackson quit school and, like many other girls in Pinching Town, went to work as a laundress. "I worked ten hours a day and I got to be a real good laundress," she wrote in her autobiography. "I could iron a man's shirt in three minutes and I was good at all those embroidered napkins and linen things." Just before her 15th birthday, she joined a procession of friends from Mount Moriah Mission Baptist Church to the Mississippi River, where she was baptized.

Jackson was a lively, intelligent teenager who grew up fast. Curious about life and the temptations offered by the rich social life in New Orleans, she found herself in a series of heated battles with her strict and uncompromising Aunt Duke. The first confrontation came when Jackson stayed out late one night in 1927 to watch the festivities at the Mardi Gras, an annual carnival held in New Orleans. She inadvertently got caught in a street riot and came in late with her clothes torn. Furious, Aunt Duke threw her out of the house, and Jackson had to spend the night with her aunt Bessie.

A few months later, Jackson stayed out late to join the second line at a brass band's funeral march. When a fight erupted, she joined in to help a friend and returned home bruised and dirty. Once again, she was thrown out of the house.

The last straw came a few weeks later, at a neighborhood party, when one of Jackson's female cousins was struggling with the unwanted advances

A baptism in the Mississippi River in the 1930s. Churchgoing blacks tended to see gospel music as a celebration of the sacred and jazz and blues as a celebration of the profane.

of a local boy. Jackson grabbed an ice pick and stabbed the youth. There were no serious injuries, but when Aunt Duke heard about the incident, she kicked Jackson out yet again.

"All right, baby," Aunt Bessie told Jackson. "If you gone, you gone." This time there would be no apologizing, no making up, and no returning. Barely 15 years old, Jackson was now on her own. She found a tiny house, with just one room and a kitchen, two blocks from Aunt Duke's and rented it for six dollars a month. Jackson furnished the house with an old iron bed and mat-

tress that she borrowed from Aunt Bessie. Then she set out to find a better job.

But the only work Jackson landed was a series of one-day jobs. Regardless of how much she liked to sing, she never thought about making a living from singing. "I could have gone into that world as a young singer," she wrote, "but it was full of wildness and things I'd been taught to believe were wrong, and it frightened me." Instead, she thought about becoming a nurse.

"We all was grieving for her," Jackson's aunt Bessie later told writer Laur-

A family from the rural South upon arriving in Chicago in the 1920s. Jackson, like hundreds of thousands of blacks who migrated north during this period, moved to Chicago in 1927.

Chicago's South Side in the 1930s, then as now a sprawling black neighborhood in the Midwest's largest city. Jackson lived with her aunt Hannah in a large South Side house.

raine Goreau. "All the time, from one house to another. They knew she was a good girl, they knew she wasn't one to get money any way she can." Worried about Mahala's future, the church secretary took it upon herself to write to Jackson's aunt Alice, who had moved to Chicago, in the hope that she might take in the teenager.

As it turned out, Jackson went to Chicago to live with her aunt Hannah instead. Jackson's uncle Emmanuel Paul had moved to the midwestern city in the mid-1920s. "When he came home to visit," Jackson later wrote, "he told us how a colored person could go shopping in white people's stores and how a negro woman could try on a dress and mix with white people. . . . For a long time we could hardly believe it was true that colored people could live that way." By early 1927, his sisters Hannah and Alice had also made the move to Chicago.

When Aunt Hannah arrived for a visit around Thanksgiving in 1927, she invited Jackson to return with her to Chicago. The 15 year old jumped at the chance. A day later, she boarded the Illinois Central—a train that would later become known as "The City of New Orleans"—with her aunt and be-

gan the journey north. In doing so, they were following in the footsteps of thousands of other southern blacks who had decided to head for industrial centers in the North, where there was the promise of better jobs, nicer homes, and greater opportunities.

The route to Chicago was especially well worn during the 1920s by a num-

ber of New Orleans musicians, including King Oliver, Jelly Roll Morton, and cornetist Louis Armstrong. In the Windy City, they found an eager audience for their exciting new music, which often meant steady work and a record contract. At the same time that these artists were bringing the sounds of New Orleans jazz to Chicago, Jackson was poised to bring the soulful sounds of southern gospel to the big northern city.

Jackson arrived in Chicago just as winter was setting in, and the first thing she noticed was how cold it was in the North; the icy wind whipped off Lake Michigan with a knifelike sharpness that literally took her breath away.

Jackson with the great jazz trumpeter Louis Armstrong in the 1960s. Armstrong was already drawing large crowds in Chicago when young Jackson moved to the city.

The second thing she observed was that a black, such as Aunt Hannah, could walk over to a taxi driven by a white and get in the car. "Down in New Orleans," Jackson wrote in her autobiography, "you'd never go near a white man's taxi."

When the taxi finally pulled up to 3250 Prairie Avenue on Chicago's South Side, Jackson was even more surprised. Behind an ornate iron fence was a tall, imposing building—nothing at all like the tiny shacks in which most blacks lived in New Orleans.

40

Aunt Hannah's apartment was big and clean, and Jackson moved into a room with one of her cousins. Eventually, she began to explore her new neighborhood and was amazed at what she saw.

At that time, more than 300,000 blacks lived in Chicago, making it the second-largest black population in the nation. (Only New York, with its black Harlem district, was home to more blacks.) Most blacks in Chicago lived on the South Side, which stretched for nearly 40 blocks—almost 7 miles—and was bounded on the east by the lakefront neighborhoods inhabited by whites and on the west by huge stockyards. According to Jackson, on the South Side "you could go for miles and miles without seeing a white person."

People from both races, however, flocked to State Street, where at places such as the Dreamland Café, the Plantation Café, and the Sunset Cabaret they could hear the hot jazz sounds of Louis Armstrong, Joe Oliver, pianist Earl "Fatha" Hines, and clarinetist Jimmy Noone. Although Jackson was too young to take in much of this, she attended some of the vaudeville shows put on every night at both the Royal Gardens and the Grande Theater.

One night shortly after she arrived in Chicago, Jackson learned that Bessie Smith was to appear at a local theater. To make sure that she got a ticket, Jackson arrived early for the show. She was not disappointed by her long wait in line. She said later that Smith "filled the whole place with her voice." In fact, Jackson was so stunned by the blues singer's performance that she remained in her seat long after the show was over. She left the theater only after the ushers told her they had to lock up for the night.

Remembering her ambition to become a nurse, Jackson enrolled in school once again. But she was forced to drop out almost immediately because Aunt Hannah became ill. Anxious to contribute to the household, Jackson filled in at Hannah's job, working as a cook in a white family's home on the North Side. A short time later, she found a job of her own, also doing housework for a well-to-do white family. She earned one dollar per day plus carfare for her efforts.

In spite of keeping a busy schedule, Jackson remained homesick for New Orleans. To help ease her feelings, Jackson's aunts took her to the large church they attended, the Greater Salem Baptist Church. Both the preacher and choir director welcomed her, and soon her big voice was booming from the choir loft. Although people occasionally made fun of her New Orleans accent and "down home" ways, she began to make new friends and feel at home in Chicago.

Among the people Jackson befriended at the Greater Salem Baptist Church were Louise Lemon and Robert, Prince, and Wilbur Johnson—the three sons of one of the church's founders—who sang as a quartet and performed religious skits at the church. Robert wrote most of their scripts, took the male leads, and directed the pageants, and Prince accompanied them on the piano, setting the tempo with a hot boogie style that owed more than a little to the State Street jazzmen. Soon, the Johnsons asked Jackson to join them, and by 1929 she found herself a member of a group that came to be called the Johnson Gospel Singers.

The group started off by writing short plays and then performing them at church socials. These moralistic pieces had titles such as *Hellbound, From Earth to Glory,* and *The Fatal Wedding.* Robert usually cast himself as the hus-

In the 1930s many jazz greats performed at the South Side's Plantation Café. Jackson, meanwhile, was embarking on her career as a gospel singer.

band, with Jackson as the wife. "We cut up and had wonderful times," Jackson said later, "and everybody enjoyed watching us." Eventually, the group branched out to singing. "With Prince at the piano, we had a bounce that made us popular from the start," Jackson recalled. "We improved on the music and strayed from the score and gave our own way to each song."

As the group became better known, it began to sing for money at other churches on the South Side. Sometimes, people in the audience were asked to donate whatever amount they wished; at other times, a small admission was charged at the door. During one of their first performances in a large church, they were shocked to hear the pastor get up after their show and condemn them for their "twisting" and "jazz." Jackson lost her temper. "This is the way we *sing* down south," she shouted back. "I been singing this way all my life in church!"

The pastor's reaction notwithstanding, most people liked the young, exciting group of singers. By 1932, the year Jackson turned 20, the Johnson Gospel Singers were getting invitations to sing in churches in southern Illinois and Indiana—hundreds of miles from Chicago—and were asked to perform at the big annual Baptist conventions in St. Louis and Cleveland. On the average, each member of the group made $1.50 per night, which was not a bad wage at the time.

On those nights when they were not performing in public, the group members usually gathered at Aunt Hannah's apartment to practice. A frequent topic of discussion was whether or not to make the group a full-time affair. One of the first organized gospel groups to travel around from church to church and from town to town, the Johnson Gospel Singers did not know if such an enterprise would succeed.

More and more, as the Johnson Gospel Singers featured Jackson in solo numbers, she became used to fans coming up to her after the show and complimenting her on her singing. One day, flush with an especially good evening's payment, she decided to spend four dollars and pay for an audition with a well-known voice teacher named Professor Kendricks. She and a friend went to Kendricks's South Side studio, where after a couple of botched attempts to adjust to the stiff, polite rhythm of the professor's pianist, Jackson stopped in frustration. The professor then showed the young singer how the spiritual was supposed to sound on the concert stage: slow and dignified, with the words precisely enunciated. "Young woman, you've got to stop that hollering," Kendricks told Jackson. "That's no way to develop a voice. . . . White people would never understand you."

A lesser spirit might have been crushed by Kendricks's comment, but not Jackson. After she left the studio, she turned to her friend and said, "I'm not studying about his high-class stuff! I'm not singing for white people! I'm singing in the church, for myself!" It was an important realization, as well as an artistic declaration of independence.

Jackson at age 17. While a young woman, Jackson won renown in Chicago's black churches as a rising gospel star.

FOUR

South Side Dreams

At the same time that she was performing with the Johnson Gospel Singers in the early 1930s, Mahala Jackson was starting to work with another person who would have a great influence on her career: Thomas A. Dorsey, the so-called father of black gospel music. The son of a Georgia preacher, he came to Chicago in the 1920s to make a living as a blues pianist and jazz composer. Known then as "Georgia Tom," he worked with some of the greatest blues singers of the day, including Ma Rainey, and forged several hit records. But by 1929, he had decided to return to his first love, gospel music.

The new gospel songs that Dorsey wrote were quite different from the older hymns and spirituals with which he had grown up. Many of his melodies were borrowed from blues songs, and his lyrics were simple, direct, and full of images of everyday life. His most popular song was "Precious Lord, Take My Hand." Written in 1932, while he was in mourning over his wife's death, the lyrics illustrate how he personalized gospel music:

> Precious Lord, take my hand,
> Lead me on, let me stand,
> I am tired, I am weak, I am worn.
> Through the storm, through the night,
> Lead me on to the light,
> Take my hand, precious Lord, lead me
> on.

Dorsey debated about whether or not it would be better to change the title phrase to "Blessed Lord," but friends dissuaded him from doing so. A sugary word like "precious," the idea of taking hands, and the short, repetitive

Jackson, accompanied by Thomas A. Dorsey, considered the father of black gospel music. Jackson started performing his songs in 1930.

phrases—all of these touches came from popular music and helped make the song speak directly to the millions of black people struggling to make ends meet during the hard times of the 1930s, when the Great Depression took hold. The more conservative churches were cautious about such new songs, however, and Dorsey worked hard to promote them.

In the process of publicizing his efforts, Dorsey helped create the professional gospel singer, one who performed at concerts where admission was charged. Up until then, gospel music was mainly sung in churches, by vocalists who performed only out of love for the music and a desire to celebrate God. The Johnson Gospel Singers had made some movement toward becoming a professional group, but not as much as Dorsey had. Beginning in 1932, he toured the country with singers he had trained and staged concerts featuring his new gospel music. He charged admission—anywhere from 1 to 10 cents—and augmented his income by selling the sheet music to his songs for 5 cents a copy.

In this area, too, Dorsey was a pioneer. Gospel songs had previously been published in songbooks and controlled by publishing companies. Borrowing another idea from popular commercial music, Dorsey published his songs on separate sheets and sold them directly to the public. Realizing that gospel singers seldom sang music exactly as it was written, he always tried to find singers to travel with him to "demonstrate" the songs to his customers.

Dorsey first heard Mahala Jackson in 1928, shortly after she came to Chicago. "She had a voice that nobody ever had or anybody ever will have," Dorsey told Laurraine Goreau. "The trills, tones, spirit. She enjoyed her religion. That was the key, the core." When he began to look in the early 1930s for singers to demonstrate his songs, Jackson was one of the people he approached. "Mahalia would stand on a street corner and demonstrate [a new song]," Dorsey said, "then we'd sell a batch: 10 cents each."

Jackson liked Dorsey's new gospel songs and soon added them to her repertoire. Up until then, she had taken most of her songs from *Gospel Pearls*, a little 1921 songbook published by the National Baptist Convention. The tunes in this book were mostly older hymns and spirituals from the 1800s—songs she had grown up with, songs that were considered proper for church. In Dorsey's songs, she heard a touch of the old New Orleans jazz bands and of the blues favored by Bessie Smith. Yet Dorsey's songs also had a strong religious message. To Jackson, they seemed to represent the best of both worlds.

In addition to performing with the Johnson Gospel Singers, Jackson had also been working as a solo act for some time. In 1930, she volunteered to sing for a revival preacher who had pitched his tent on a vacant lot near her apartment. That same year, she began singing with the Reverend Mr. Seals, who worked out of the Pilgrim Baptist Church near her home. She sang not

Chicago's Edgewater Beach Hotel, on the shores of Lake Michigan, where Jackson worked as a maid while making her name as a gospel singer.

only in church but in hospitals, reform schools, and prison cells—wherever the reverend took his ministry. In 1931, a local politician named Louie B. Anderson, who had heard Jackson at the tent revival, hired her to sing at his political rallies. The next summer, an even more powerful politician, William Dawson, ran for Congress, and he, too, hired Jackson.

"I sang for I don't know *how* many of those meetings a night," Jackson told Laurraine Goreau. "I was rather gifted at changing words." Instead of singing "Jesus has brought us all the way," she would sing, "Dawson has brought us all the way." Like Anderson, Dawson was elected to office, and Jackson began to appreciate how gospel music could be used as a tool for political change. It was a lesson she would remember in later years, when she worked in the civil rights movement with the Reverend Martin Luther King, Jr.

After singing at political functions, Jackson soon got an even more interesting offer. The owner of a neighborhood funeral home, Robert H. Miller, asked her to become a regular performer at the funeral services he held. When he told her that he would pay two dollars for each performance, which was good money in those days, Jackson became elated. Soon, she was calling Miller "my manager," and he was happy to act as one. On nights when there were no funerals, he would use the "family car" from the funeral home to drive Jackson to concert dates he had set up. Most of these dates were at churches around Chicago, but some took place in school auditoriums and thus constituted Jackson's first concerts outside a church. When the concert was held in nearby cities or in the suburbs, Miller would charge admission, anywhere from 25 to 50 cents.

Miller even took Jackson into a recording studio and made a series of "custom-pressed" records. Instead of being financed by a commercial record company, these discs were completely bought and paid for by the artist. Miller sold the records at the National Baptist Convention as a way of advertising his new star. They were Jackson's first records. Very few of them were made, however, and today they are among gospel's rarest and most valuable records.

All of this was happening during some of the hardest times in modern history: the Great Depression. In October 1929, the price of stocks on the New York Stock Exchange dropped suddenly, setting off a rapid and calamitous chain reaction: Banks closed, businesses failed, and millions lost their jobs. The blacks who had moved to northern cities were especially hard hit; their relatives who had stayed on farms in the South could at least raise enough food for themselves in their gardens.

Sheet music for a Jackson standard. She was known for transforming old gospel songs through subtle emotional shadings.

Unemployed Chicagoans living in tar-paper shacks in 1932. The Great Depression, which ravaged the world economy for a decade, hit black Americans particularly hard.

That was not possible in Chicago. "On the South Side it was as if somebody had pulled a switch and everything had stopped running," Jackson wrote in her autobiography. The mills and factories that had attracted blacks to the North were closing right and left. "Suddenly the streets were full of men and women who'd been put out of their jobs," Jackson recalled. "All day long you'd see crowds of them shuffling back and forth and standing on street corners." When people could not pay their rent, they were evicted from their apartments and houses. "The city parks were full of people living in shanties made out of tin and wood scraps," Jackson said. "The Depression made the South Side a place of broken hopes and dreams." She was hardly surprised when the collection plate passed at her church concerts often came back with only a couple of nickels or dimes. The 1930s was not a good time to be starting a career of any sort, let alone one like gospel singing.

Dividing her time between the Johnson Gospel Singers and engagements with Robert Miller and Thomas A. Dorsey, Jackson was able to keep her career going, although she was still a long way from making a real living at it. During a good week, her singing could earn her as much as $10, which meant that she still had to work at day jobs. She did housework for a time, then worked in a date-packing factory. Finally, she found a fairly well paying job at the plush Edgewater Beach Hotel on the shores of Lake Michigan, where she spent her days as a maid. At night and on weekends, she stepped neatly into her other role, that of a rising gospel star, the focus of applause in dozens of churches and school auditoriums.

Although Jackson's busy schedule did not leave her very much time for socializing, she dated occasionally and had her share of admirers and boyfriends. She was not prepared, though, for what happened one evening at a social held at the Greater Salem Baptist Church. There she met a quiet, dignified, well-dressed man around 30 years old. Isaac Lane Grey Hockenhull was a southerner—he was originally from a small town in Mississippi—and a college graduate with a degree from Tuskegee Institute and additional credentials from Fisk University. The depression had taken him down a peg, forcing him to work as a mail carrier for the post office, but it had not changed his impeccable manners and smooth style. "He took himself and life very seriously," Jackson recalled. "And he had a speaking voice that called for you to listen to him even if he was only telling you to pass the potatoes."

When Ike Hockenhull asked Jackson out, she at first did not take him seri-

Jackson married her first husband, Ike Hockenhull, in 1936. Their marriage fell apart because of her travel schedule and his gambling at the racetrack.

ously. "I couldn't believe that this educated man who was ten years older than me really could be interested in a girl who never knew any school after the eighth grade," she wrote. He soon convinced her, however, and before long he was squiring her to movies, vaudeville shows, and church socials. He sent her candy and flowers and became a favorite with Aunt Hannah and Aunt Bell. He introduced her to his mother, who made and sold special cosmetics from old secret recipes. Soon, Jackson was taking along a suitcase full of cosmetics to sell on the side when she went out to perform at concerts. It was of little surprise to anybody when, in 1936, after a year's courtship, Hockenhull and Jackson were married.

Although Hockenhull loved Jackson's singing, from the start of their marriage he resented the many trips his new bride made so that she could perform at concerts. He was also concerned about the type of music she was singing. "Ike loved me, but he didn't love my songs," Jackson recalled in her autobiography. "He was educated and he thought gospel singing wasn't. He wanted me to be a concert singer. He wanted me to take voice training, and he and I were always fussing about it."

The situation became worse when jazz greats such as Louis Armstrong and Earl Hines came by the apartment to ask Jackson to join their respective bands as a singer. Both bands had garnered national reputations while appearing on radio shows and winning lucrative record contracts. "I *know* what you can do with the blues," Armstrong told her. "Make you some real green." The offer was tempting, but Jackson said no.

A few months later, Jackson was confronted by a far more serious temptation. Hockenhull was temporarily laid off at the post office at the same time that Jackson's church concert bookings hit a dry spell. One evening, the young couple found themselves with a total of 60 cents to their name. In desperation, Hockenhull showed his wife a newspaper ad for a new show that was looking for singers. It was a stage show sponsored by the Federal Theater Project, part of a government agency designed to help actors, actresses, stagehands, musicians, and writers get work during the depression. Entitled *The Hot Mikado*, it was to be a jazz version of a well-known British operetta, with an all-black cast. Against her better judgment but driven by the need to bring in some money, Jackson agreed to go.

At the audition, Jackson tried to sing something from her little gospel songbook, *Gospel Pearls*, but the producers told her she had to sing from sheet music. She left the theater, spent her last bit of money on the sheet music for "Sometimes I Feel Like a Motherless Child"—a song that was contained in *Gospel Pearls*—and returned to the audition. As she blundered her way through the unfamiliar sheet music arrangement, she felt guilty about what she was doing. "I was chancing my soul for a dollar," she remembered, "and it was just like hot grease popping at me to hear people in that auditorium applaud." Jackson was offered the part—at the heady wage of $60 a week—and decided to take it. She had no other choice.

That evening, though, Ike came home with some news of his own: He had found a job selling insurance. It was like a sign from God. "Thank you, Jesus," a relieved Jackson exclaimed. "I don't have to go on the stage!"

Jackson performs in a Chicago church. In the late 1930s and into the 1940s, Jackson made the leap from church singing to commercial records.

FIVE

"Move on Up
a Little Higher"

Mahala Jackson's fame spread slowly but steadily during the mid-1930s. By then, she was traveling well outside the Chicago circuit, taking trains to appearances in black churches from New York to California. On May 21, 1937, she recorded two songs, "God Shall Wipe All Tears Away" and "Keep Me Every Day," for Decca Records, the nation's third-largest record company.

But the records did not sell well, and the company soon dropped her contract. Although she was becoming well known on the gospel circuit, she was still what people then called a "fish-and-bread" singer. "I was singing for my supper as well as for the Lord," Jackson explained. "The little churches would send for me and then pass me along from one to another. The minister's family would give me a room and

something to eat, and then we would divide the admission money, part for the church and part for my carfare and pocket money."

It was at about this time that Jackson, as a concession to show business, decided to add an *i* to her first name, turning "Mahala" into "Mahalia." The change illustrated how much she wanted to push her career beyond the traditional gospel circuit.

There was also a change in her personal life. In 1934, Jackson took into her home an eight-year-old boy named John Sellers. He was something of a street beggar, who had come up and tugged on her coattails one day to tell her how much he liked her singing. The boy, as it turned out, was a pretty good singer himself. Jackson insisted that he go to school, but in the evenings

The Golden Gate Quintet, one of many gospel groups that sprang up on small, independent record labels during World War II.

she taught him about singing. By 1937, he was performing with Jackson at tent revivals and was widely regarded as her protégé.

Meanwhile, the relationship between Jackson and her husband began to deteriorate. The church had never played a large part in Ike Hockenhull's life, and he could not understand why his wife continued to turn down offers to sing jazz or blues in favor of gospel music. Nor was he enamored of Jackson's long trips on the fish-and-bread circuit.

At some point, Hockenhull became interested in horse racing and started going to the track to make bets on what he regarded as "sure things." Although he proved to be skilled at playing the horses, he occasionally lost a good deal of money. It got so that Jackson was never sure whether she would come home to "chicken" (a bankroll won by her husband) or "feathers" (no money at all). His gambling problem added to the couple's troubles, and in 1941 they agreed to divorce.

By then, Chicago's South Side was the center of the revolution in gospel music that was sweeping the country. It was also the home of several music publishing companies specializing in the new gospel sounds. At the heart of the revolution was Jackson's old friend, Thomas A. Dorsey. Working with a singer named Sallie Martin, he had moved beyond selling sheet music and writing new songs. In 1933, Dorsey began organizing gospel choirs—groups of singers who performed his new, lively music and his blues-tinged songs—all over the South Side. As the decade continued, Dorsey and Martin set up similar groups in Cleveland, Philadelphia, Los Angeles, and many other cities in the South and Midwest.

Other composers and singers, such as Roberta Martin (no relation to Sallie), followed suit by organizing gospel choirs in Chicago. Although little of this new music was recorded, these groups sometimes performed live for radio audiences. The Roberta Martin Singers, appearing on live radio, eventually had a big hit with their arrangement of the spiritual "Didn't It Rain," which Jackson later recorded and made into a hit of her own.

The older, more conservative churches were reluctant to embrace the new gospel music. But as the Great Depression cut into church attendance—and the amount of donations made by the congregation—churches found that appearances by Jackson, Dorsey, and their colleagues were a way to get people back into the pews.

In 1939, Dorsey invited Jackson to travel with him to demonstrate his new songs. He liked her vocal style (and would later write a song, "Peace in the Valley," just for her). Although Dorsey's offer meant uncertain wages, long train rides, and having to spend most weekends away from home—hardly the way to patch up her then-failing marriage—she jumped at the chance. She relished the chance to perform Dorsey's songs.

Moreover, Jackson could afford to take a little gamble of her own. She had recently opened up her own business, Mahalia's Beauty Salon, and with hundreds of her fans flocking to the salon, it immediately proved successful. Soon, she needed to have five women working there to accommodate the influx of customers.

Thus, Jackson settled into a pattern that served her well through the early 1940s: As the nation became unsettled

The sheet music for "Move on Up a Little Higher." Jackson recorded the song in 1947 and made it a huge hit, selling 2 million records.

by World War II, a growing number of people turned to gospel music for spiritual comfort. Wartime shortages led to travel restrictions, however, that made it increasingly hard for Jackson and Dorsey to take their music to other cities. So, when Jackson received an offer to become choir director of the St. Luke Baptist Church just around the corner from her home, she left Dorsey's entourage and accepted the post.

Even though gospel music was becoming ever more popular, the larger record companies showed little faith in gospel music as a commercial venture. Smaller companies were willing to give it a chance, though. One such company was Apollo Records, a New York–based outfit run by Bess Berman, who would eventually help Jackson attain national prominence.

In September 1946, Jackson received a startling offer from Johnny Meyers, who liked to promote gospel concerts in a big way—not just in churches or schoolhouses but in huge venues. One of his favorite places to put on a concert was the Golden Gate Ballroom in New York, a large hall that usually featured jazz one week and gospel extravaganzas the next. Meyers offered to pay Jackson $1,000 in cash to hold a concert there. Amazed at the amount, she quickly accepted.

Bess Berman was in the audience that night, and Jackson's vocals left her deeply impressed. But as much as Berman liked Jackson's voice, there was one hitch: Berman was nervous about having Jackson record gospel songs. Even though the record buyers that Berman targeted were black—Apollo's catalog consisted mostly of records by popular jazz and rhythm-and-blues bands—the company had recorded a couple of gospel acts but had enjoyed little commercial success with them.

At a meeting the next day in the Apollo office, Berman asked Jackson whether she would be interested in recording a few blues songs. When the vocalist replied that she would not, an awkward silence followed. Finally, Berman said, "All right, we'll try you. Four sides." For the third time in her career, Jackson got prepared to enter a recording studio. She hoped this time would be the charm.

Working with Apollo's music director and arranger, Art Freeman, Jackson went into a New York studio in early October and cut four songs. Accompanied only by a pianist, she sang some of her concert favorites, including "I'm Gonna Tell God All About It One of These Days":

> I'm gonna tell Him how my friends and
>   enemies
> Brought me to my bended knees,
> And the doors that were open for me
> Sometimes closed, Lord, in my face.

Jackson might very well have been singing of her own years of frustration at trying to make it as a gospel singer. "I'm Gonna Tell God All About It One of These Days" would be the first of many records she would make in which she injected hints of her own personal life into the songs she performed.

Released in November 1946, the record did not sell especially well, although a popular Chicago disc jockey named Studs Terkel played it repeatedly on his jazz show. For the first time ever, a large white audience heard Jackson's voice, as Terkel played the record over and over, until he wore it out. Unfortunately, Terkel was almost alone in his enthusiasm for the new singer, and when Apollo released Jackson's second record in May 1947, it, too, failed to attract much attention.

*Jackson with two young visitors. In the second half of her career,
Jackson devoted much of her energy to young people.*

Looking over the sales figures for Jackson's records in New York, Berman shook her head and told Freeman to terminate Jackson's contract. But Freeman was not so sure; he hated to give up on that incredible voice. He remembered that during her first recording session, Jackson had warmed up with a song called "Move on Up a Little Higher." Everyone had liked that song, but it was too long. Her rendition ran about five minutes, and the average time for a single in the late 1940s was only three minutes. Freeman thought he had the solution: Break the song into two sections and issue them on separate sides of the single as parts one and two. A skeptical Berman agreed to

give it a try, and Freeman called up Jackson to set up a recording session.

The call came at a bad time for Jackson. In order to make the recording session, she would have to rush home from Kansas City, where she was scheduled to sing at the National Baptist Convention. She would also have to find some backup musicians in a hurry. Yet she agreed to do it.

In forming a group to back her up, Jackson settled on James Lee, a singer she sometimes worked with who also played piano in a simple but effective style. He had just gotten out of the army, and he arrived in Chicago only a day before the session was to take place. "I don't even know what you're

The Greater Salem Baptist Church on Chicago's South Side, Jackson's home church.

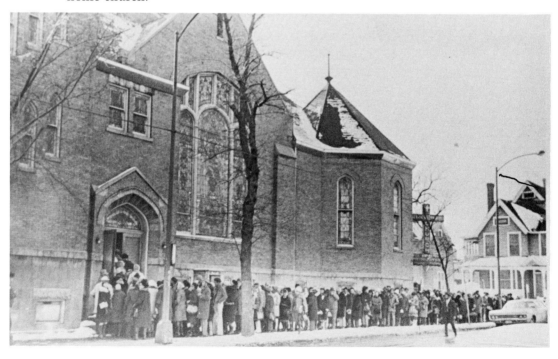

going to record," Lee told Jackson, who decided to fill out her sound with an organ and chose an old friend from the neighborhood, James Francis, to do so. The three of them practiced at St. Luke Baptist Church all day and into the night. At three o'clock in the morning, they finally decided they were ready to cut the record.

"Move on Up a Little Higher" was not a new song. It had been written in the mid-1940s by the Reverend W. Herbert Brewster, a Memphis composer who rivaled Thomas A. Dorsey for the title of most influential gospel writer. Brewster had grown up in rural Tennessee but as a young man moved to Memphis, where he heard the same kind of blues that Jackson had enjoyed in New Orleans. He idolized Mamie Smith, Ma Rainey, Bessie Smith, and Memphis's own blues composer, W. C. Handy. Brewster favored long songs, full of images from black folklore and everyday life. "A gospel song is a sermon set to music," he once explained.

"Move on Up a Little Higher" was introduced to the public by one of Brewster's singers, Queen C. Anderson, a popular singer in the South. One night in the mid-1940s, Jackson shared a concert stage with Anderson and heard "Move on Up." She immediately liked it and started singing it as well. Later, when Art Freeman heard her singing it to herself—"to cheer myself up," she told him, "to give me courage"—she performed it more slowly than anybody else did, transforming it into a warm, comforting tune.

Jackson singing at the Greater Salem Baptist Church. With the success of "Move on Up," she replaced many of her appearances at churches with concert hall dates.

They embellished the song a bit in the studio. Lee started it off with a medium rocking tempo on the piano. Then the organ joined in; next came Jackson. Her voice was strong and clear, and at once she began to orna-

Thomas A. Dorsey in 1979. His collaboration with Jackson formally began in 1939, when she went on the road as a "demonstrator" of Dorsey's sheet music.

ment the melody with little blues notes. Her accompanists knew she was not performing the song exactly as Brewster had written it, but of course few gospel singers did—that was what made them special.

As Jackson moved into the second part of the song, she even began to change some of the words from the original version. Brewster's lyrics were

Soon as these feet strike Zion,
I'm gonna lay down my heavy burden,
Gonna put on my robe in glory,
Gonna shout and tell the story,
I've been coming over hills and mountains,
Gonna drink from the crystal fountain,
All God's sons and daughters,
Will be drinking that old healing water.

Jackson pared down the lyrics, which resulted in a slightly less emphatic version:

Soon as my feet strike Zion,
Lay down my heavy burden,
Lord, put on my robe out in glory, oh Lord,
Sing and tell the story,
Come over hills and mountains, Lord,
Up to the Christian fountain,
All God's sons and daughters, Lord,
Drinking that old healing water.

On she went, chorus after chorus, each verse building in intensity. Afterward, Freeman came out of the control booth with a big smile on his face.

Jackson went home that morning and fell back into her routine of going to the beauty shop and singing at church.

She never imagined what was about to happen next.

When Apollo released the two-sided "Move on Up" in December 1947, the record took the South Side by storm. In that area alone, 50,000 copies were sold in the first 4 weeks it was out. Soon, the record was in demand all across the country. Apollo's pressing plant could not fill all of its orders for the records. Eventually, Apollo decided to stop pressing other performers' records so more of Jackson's discs could be produced. Each day, Berman shipped a number of records to Jackson in Chicago, who then delivered them personally to the local record stores.

The sudden success of "Move on Up" prompted Decca Records to rush out a cover version, a close imitation of the song, in an attempt to cash in on the success of the original. When a big record company like Decca did this, it usually sounded the death knell for sales of the smaller label's version. But Bess Berman fought back. She managed to book Jackson to perform at a convention of jukebox dealers in Chicago. Jukeboxes accounted for a lot of record sales, and when the dealers heard Jackson singing "Move on Up" in person, they had no doubt as to whose record they wanted to stock.

"Move on Up" went on to sell 2 million copies. It was by far the biggest hit any gospel singer had ever had. Suddenly, within the span of only a few weeks, Mahalia Jackson was a nationally known singing star. Her career, and the gospel music on which it was founded, was about to go into high gear.

Jackson in the 1950s, years marked by growing fame and her new role as legitimizer of gospel's place in mainstream American music.

SIX

"The World's Greatest Gospel Singer"

After the success of "Move on Up," Bess Berman set up Jackson with a manager, Harry Lenetska, a veteran of the New York show business scene. Now, for the first time in her career, Jackson had someone to handle her concert bookings, promotions, and scheduling. Lenetska had worked with some of the nation's biggest stars, including vocalists Ella Fitzgerald, Sophie Tucker, and the Ink Spots, as well as with television impresario Ed Sullivan.

Lenetska had experience, contacts, and faith in Jackson's potential. He was the kind of manager who could get his clients lucrative bookings. He did things in a big way. In April 1948, for instance, when Jackson returned to New York for a concert, she was amazed to see her name lit up by huge neon signs on Broadway. Offers for her to sing were coming in so fast Lenetska barely had time to schedule them. The owner of a popular New York night spot offered her $5,000 for a week-long engagement, but Jackson drew the line at singing in clubs. Nevertheless, she was quickly learning one thing about the commercial music world of the late 1940s: Hit records were nice, but the real money came from personal appearances.

Jackson's new whirlwind schedule had its low points, however. Once, in Philadelphia, she got into a dispute with a promoter who refused to give her a share of the gate. Jackson walked into the ticket office, scooped the money into her purse, and left for her hotel. The promoter swore out an arrest warrant, and the next morning the local

Chicago disc jockey and writer Studs Terkel, who wrote for Jackson's radio show, with pianist Chet Roble. Terkel was an avid booster of Jackson's early records.

police brought Jackson out of her hotel room in handcuffs. The incident was soon straightened out, but it made Jackson even more suspicious about the world of professional entertainment.

Yet the high points outweighed the low ones. In June 1950, Jackson appeared at a huge concert in Houston, Texas, where more than 5,000 people had paid to hear her sing. Later that year, New York promoter Joe Bostic set up a concert for her at prestigious Car-

negie Hall. It was to be the first all-gospel program ever held at America's most widely celebrated concert hall. Jackson had her doubts about the show. She told Bostic, "These types of songs are not high enough for Carnegie Hall. *Carnegie Hall!* That's for the great opera singers!"

Jackson worried about what dress to wear, what songs to perform, and who should accompany her. But all her worries melted away on October 1, when she walked onstage at Carnegie Hall and sang "A City Called Heaven" and "Amazing Grace" in front of 8,000 people. The next morning, the newspapers raved about her performance. One paper went so far as to call her "the incomparable Mahalia Jackson, Queen of Gospel Singers."

Along with performing in public, Jackson also spent a fair amount of time in the recording studio. Bess Berman wasted little time in getting Jackson to record several follow-ups to "Move on Up." One such song was "Even Me," which was released in January 1948 and was soon nipping at the heels of "Move on Up" as another million-seller. Then there was "How I Got Over," a song written by the Reverend W. Herbert Brewster. It was one of the first tunes Jackson recorded with the backing of a vocal group.

Jackson added to her playlist the bluesy gospel songs of young Kenneth Morris, who wrote tunes that sounded almost like rock and roll. Although many churches refused to allow these songs to be performed, Jackson admired them. She recorded Morris's "Dig a Little Deeper" in 1947 and "I Can Put My Trust in Jesus" in 1949 (the latter won an award from the French Academy in 1950 as the best jazz record of the year). In 1952, Jackson recorded "In the Upper Room," which was composed by perhaps the finest female gospel writer of the time, Lucie Campbell. It became Jackson's fourth-biggest seller, followed closely by her unique version of "Silent Night." All told, Jackson wound up recording 68 songs

for Apollo between 1946 and 1954. Almost all were issued as singles, and almost all were marketed for a black audience.

During this period, gospel music continued to move out of the churches and into the concert halls. It became a national fad—and big business. Promoters would book giant halls and convention centers and stage "battles" between two leading gospel singers or groups. New independent record companies, such as Savoy, Nashboro, Specialty, King, Duke, and Gotham, rushed into the market with hundreds of gospel recordings. Performers such as the Roberta Martin Singers, the

Jackson, always the consummate performer, at home. Her 1950 concert at New York's Carnegie Hall is considered a pivotal event in gospel history.

The Five Blind Boys of Alabama, a gospel group that first became famous in the 1950s. Often composed of more than 5 members, they were still one of gospel's top groups in the 1980s.

Golden Gate Quartet, the Pilgrim Travellers, the Five Blind Boys of Alabama, Sister Rosetta Tharpe, and Edna Gallmon Cooke traveled the gospel circuit, their hit records becoming the bread and butter of newly formed gospel radio shows.

Unlike other forms of popular music, gospel music featured equal participation by men and women. Right from the start, women played a vital role as composers, arrangers, promoters, instrumentalists, and singers. As Jackson's fame spread, she took charge of her career, letting those around her know who was calling the shots.

One of the things Jackson did was to hire a young South Side pianist named Mildred Falls as a full-time accompanist. Falls soon learned the Jackson style so well that she could anticipate almost every breath the singer took. Falls was so in tune with Jackson that she became her regular traveling companion for the next 20 years.

With all her success, Jackson's audiences in the late 1940s remained predominantly black. " 'Move on Up,' " she said, "made me famous. But only with Negroes. I still lived far inside the colored world." Even the audience at Carnegie Hall had been predominantly black. Disc jockeys who played her Apollo records, such as Studs Terkel, had to advise their white listeners that they could obtain her records only from a distributor or from record stores on the South Side.

Slowly, the extent of Jackson's appeal began to change. In September 1950, she was asked to be a guest at the newly formed Institute of Jazz Studies seminar, which was held at the Music Inn in Massachusetts. Distinguished music scholars from all over the country met there to hammer out a definition of jazz and to learn about gospel music. Over the course of a week, Jack-

Jackson was hospitalized several times for various problems. In 1952, following her first European tour, she was operated on to remove a sarcoid tumor.

son sang for them and answered their questions; they tape-recorded her songs and argued among themselves about how she made her music. After the seminar ended, one of the participants told her, "Mahalia, if you'd started out the door and down to the lake while you were singing 'Shall We Gather at the River,' all those experts would have followed you and waded right into the water to be baptized."

Mahalia Jackson was attracting a similar following in Europe, where fans and critics alike paid tribute to jazz musicians long before many Americans did. Her records won major awards in Europe, and she often received letters from France and Denmark in which her fans asked her to tour Europe. Finally, she said, "If they're going to be nice enough to give me a prize, then I ought to be enough of a lady to go over there and say thank you. But I won't be surprised if they don't get my music."

When Jackson arrived in Paris in October 1952, police were called to hold back the crowd that mobbed her. She went on to Holland, Belgium, and Denmark and encountered similar scenes. The morning after her show in Copenhagen, some of the local children filled her hotel lobby with flowers.

Such receptions certainly buoyed Jackson's spirits, because for some months she had not been feeling well. She suffered from pains, bleeding, and dizziness, but shrugged it off to meet her busy schedule. At a return engagement in Paris in December, however, it all caught up with her: She fainted onstage. Her doctors told her she could not continue the tour. She required medical attention immediately, they said. Jackson would hear none of it and climbed aboard the first plane for Chicago.

While rumors about what was wrong with Jackson abounded in public—she had a bronchial infection, she had tuberculosis, she had collapsed from nervous exhaustion—her doctors in Chicago confirmed what had been suspected in Paris: The singer had cancer. Surgery was performed to remove the tumor, and after she returned home from the hospital to recover from the ordeal, visiting friends thought she would not survive. Meanwhile, the official story given to the press was that a bronchial ailment had forced the cancellation of her tour.

One month after the surgery, Jackson's doctors announced that her X rays were clear. Things were looking up. Still, Jackson had lost an enormous amount of weight while recovering from her illness and felt that Bess Berman, Harry Lenetska, and all her other new associates in New York had written her off. Jackson prayed as never before, vowing to make a comeback.

In February 1953, Jackson was well enough to start going back to church and was able to eat some of her favorite foods, which included fresh greens, hot-water cornbread, and stewed corn. In March, she sang at some local churches—a far cry from the big halls she had been playing before she became ill, but at least it was a start. When she felt strong enough to make her first trip out of town, to Michigan, her spirits

Jackson at a recording session with Duke Ellington, the great jazz musician and bandleader who is considered one of the foremost composers in American musical history.

began to revive. In June, she contacted promoter Al Duckett and decided to prove to all of her hometown fans that she could still sing. She held a concert in Chicago Stadium, and more than 10,000 fans crowded in. That summer, she took to the road again, touring throughout the South.

Once again, Jackson did not accept every opportunity that came her way. She turned down $5,000 a week to star in a new Broadway show, *New Faces*,

71

Jackson with Ellington. Jackson was widely admired in jazz circles for her improvisatory genius.

Jackson listens to a playback during a 1950s recording session. She recorded 68 songs on Apollo Records from 1948 to 1954, then jumped to Columbia.

feeling that it crossed over her all-important line between gospel and pop music. She did agree, however, to appear at another concert in Carnegie Hall that October.

While Jackson was in New York, Berman talked her into cutting some more records, Ed Sullivan put her on his popular television show, and Louis Armstrong's agent called and asked for a chance to book her. One of the most interesting calls she received, though, came from Mitch Miller of Columbia Records. Jackson knew that Columbia was one of the country's biggest and best labels. Boasting topflight studios and engineers and an aggressive promotion department, the company managed to land its discs in every record store in the country, not just jazz stores or stores frequented by blacks.

Moreover, Columbia had just introduced a revolutionary type of record—the LP, or long-play record. Grooved at 33⅓ revolutions per minute, the LP could hold up to approximately 25 minutes of music per side and could let a song run on far longer than the old 78 rpm discs did. Jackson would never again have to split a song like she had to do with "Move on Up."

Jackson took an immediate liking to Mitch Miller and was intrigued by his interest in trying to bring gospel music to a larger audience. It took her a year of soul-searching and sifting through other offers, but late in the summer of 1954 she finally signed a contract with Columbia.

On November 22, 1954, Jackson, accompanied by Mildred Falls and Ralph Jones, walked into the big Columbia studios in New York to cut her first record for the company. One of Columbia's promotional writers had recently publicized her as "the world's greatest gospel singer." With a sigh, she set out to prove it.

In the late 1950s, Jackson, by now nationally famous, became involved in the growing civil rights movement.

SEVEN

"I Been 'Buked and
I Been Scorned"

Mahalia Jackson's contract with Columbia proved to be a major breakthrough for the singer in a number of ways. Not only did it result in a string of fine albums and singles but it also led directly to her CBS radio show, a television show, and a series of recordings with one of America's greatest bandleaders and composers, Duke Ellington. There were compromises, though. The people at Columbia often convinced her to record third-rate imitation gospel songs; ultra-slick gospel quartets were sometimes brought in to back her up; and, on occasion, large string orchestras were used to accompany her. Still, whenever Jackson toured the South and the Midwest (in her new Cadillac), she made the trip with the bare-bones minimum of one piano player.

Another thing that Jackson could not avoid, even with her newly won celebrity status, was lingering racial prejudice. In 1956, for instance, she spent Christmas in New Orleans following an appearance on a nationwide NBC television program called "Wide, Wide World." As she went shopping in the downtown streets, fans—both black and white—recognized her and offered their greetings. But when she entered a white-owned restaurant, she was refused service, and when she wanted to get a taxi, white drivers would not allow her into their cab. Racial segregation remained the (unwritten, in some cases) law of the land.

An even more dramatic episode occurred when Jackson decided to buy a house in Chicago. Although she owned her apartment house on the South Side,

Jackson moved into this house in the white Chicago neighborhood of Chatham Village in 1956 and promptly received several anonymous threats.

she still had trouble rehearsing her singing. "Even though they were my tenants," she wrote in her autobiography, "the people still came flying upstairs to scold me when I sang loud to myself." As a result, she began to look for a single-family house in the predominantly white suburbs, but every time she inquired about a house on the market, she was told that it had just been sold or that the sellers had changed their mind and had decided not to move. The people in the suburbs of Chicago, it seemed, were no more anxious to have a black neighbor than the New Orleans restaurateurs were to

have a black customer, no matter how famous she was.

Finally, Jackson found a doctor who was willing to sell her his house, which stood on the corner of 83rd and Indiana in the white Chicago neighborhood of Chatham Village. But when the other homeowners in the neighborhood found out about the sale, "the people nearly went crazy," Jackson recalled. "Everybody was holding meetings up and down the block. You'd have thought an atomic bomb was coming instead of me." Anonymous callers phoned her late at night, threatening to dynamite her house if she moved in.

"You're going to need more than gospel songs and prayers to save you," one caller vowed. She received unsigned letters that were full of hate and threats.

Undeterred, Jackson began redecorating the house in preparation for her move. A few weeks later, when she returned from a singing engagement in Cincinnati, she found that someone had fired bullets through a picture window, shattering the glass and ruining some walls as well. Furious, she called Chicago mayor Richard Daley. Within minutes, police cars sped up to the house.

When Jackson moved into the house shortly thereafter, police were still posted outside it. They would continue to guard her home for a year. When the newscaster Edward R. Murrow asked to broadcast a live interview with Jackson from her house for his "Person to Person" television program, she tried to ease things in the neighborhood by inviting all the local children to join her on the air for a cake-and-ice-cream party. Many came, but what the cameras did not show was the row of For Sale signs that lined the street outside the house.

Such incidents prompted Jackson to take some political action. Even during her earliest days in Chicago, she had not been hesitant to sing for political candidates she supported. In 1948, she had worked for Harry S. Truman's presidential campaign. In March 1956, she had performed for First Lady Mamie Eisenhower at the White House, and

Jackson entertains guests at her home, among them the singer Harry Belafonte, who, like Jackson, was one of the first celebrities to work in the civil rights movement.

Rosa Parks, the Montgomery, Alabama, woman who was the focus of the 1956 bus boycott that galvanized the black civil rights movement, arrives for arraignment at a Montgomery courthouse.

four months later she had sung at the Democratic National Convention in Chicago, at the invitation of Mayor Daley. Now Jackson began to wonder if it wasn't time to get involved in righting some of the wrongs she saw in the United States.

Three weeks after she sang at the Democratic convention, Jackson traveled to the National Baptist Convention in Denver, where she appeared annually as the convention's official soloist. But something special happened at the 1956 convention. Jackson met two black clergymen from the South who wanted to have a word with her: Martin Luther King, Jr., and Ralph David Abernathy.

Only two years earlier, the United States Supreme Court had ruled that segregation by race in public schools was a violation of the Constitution. This ruling angered conservative white communities, especially those in the South and Midwest that still maintained separate schools for blacks and whites. The Supreme Court's decision gave heart, however, to the generations of blacks who were tired of being treated as though they were second-class citizens, and they launched what came to be known as the civil rights movement.

On December 1, 1955, Rosa Parks was arrested in Montgomery, Alabama, for refusing to move to the back of a city bus simply because she was black, as was dictated by a city ordinance. About 25,000 protesters—half the black population of Montgomery—showed up at the courthouse when she was brought to trial. Soon, there was an even greater show of support for Parks. The city's blacks, organized in part by King and Abernathy, elected to boycott the public buses. To carry on the the boycott, the two men helped form the Montgomery Improvement Association, which raised money through the local churches and organized car pools so blacks could get to work without using the bus system.

When Jackson met King and Abernathy in early 1956, she was already

Jackson, long involved in the campaigns of white Democratic politicians, sings at the 1956 Democratic National Convention in Chicago.

well acquainted with King's father, a prominent Atlanta preacher, whom she had known for many years through her work at the National Baptist Convention. She listened as they explained the situation at Montgomery. The boycott had already been on for several weeks, with no end in sight, and it was important to raise funds and rally the people. Would Jackson possibly find the time to come to Montgomery and sing at a fund-raising rally? She agreed at once.

Many blacks in southern Alabama may not have been sure who King or Abernathy were, but they certainly knew who Mahalia Jackson was. When they heard about the big rally, which was held at a local church, they began pouring into town hours before the eight o'clock starting time. Loudspeakers were set up outside the church to accommodate the overflow crowd. Police turned out in force as angry whites jeered and taunted.

The rally and concert went off without any disruption, and Jackson returned to Chicago feeling good about her contribution to the cause. Later on,

Jackson with President Dwight D. Eisenhower. In March 1956, Jackson gave her first performance at the White House.

Jackson at the 1961 inauguration ball with the daughters of Vice-president Lyndon B. Johnson, Lucy Baines (left) and Lynda Bird.

however, she learned that two days after she left Abernathy's house, where she had stayed while she was in Montgomery, a bomb had exploded, wrecking Abernathy's living room and the bedroom where Jackson had slept.

Over the next few years, Jackson became good friends with King, who quickly emerged as the leader of the civil rights movement. She often sang at fund-raising rallies, and whenever King came to Chicago, he and his associates usually met at her Chatham Village house to plan strategy and enjoy Jackson's home cooking. After the Montgomery boycott was won, King organized the Southern Christian Leadership Conference, which he dedicated to winning the civil rights struggle throughout the South.

King himself was fond of gospel music and made it a central part of his campaign. Jackson pitched in as well. At her concerts in the late 1950s, she often sang "We Shall Overcome," the unofficial anthem of the civil rights movement, and the older hymn from which it was derived, "I'll Be All Right."

Jackson supervises civil rights workers in her Chicago home. Jackson met Martin Luther King, Jr., the leader of the movement, in 1956.

Soon, other songs from black gospel tradition, such as "Go Down, Moses," "I'm on My Way," and "Go Tell It on the Mountain," were being sung around the South during civil rights marches. Jackson would later devote an entire album to the favorite hymns of Martin Luther King, Jr.

One night in 1960, shortly after John F. Kennedy was elected president of the United States, his brother-in-law, film star Peter Lawford, called Jackson. A big inaugural celebration was being planned in Washington, D.C., and the inauguration committee, headed by entertainer Frank Sinatra, wanted her to sing "The Star-Spangled Banner." Although she had never sung the national anthem in public before, she agreed to the request.

On January 20, 1961, at the Armory in Washington, D.C., the inaugural gala got under way with Jackson singing the national anthem for the new president. Because Jackson always sang with her eyes shut, she had no idea of how she was being received. But later that night, the president himself came over to her and thanked her for singing. He even went so far as to tell her that he had enjoyed her work for years. "He made me feel as if I was part of his life and time," she said.

During the next three years, the civil rights movement, supported by the Kennedy administration, made even more headway. As busy as Jackson was in making new recordings and traveling to concert sites across the country, she often managed to turn up at King-led rallies. The crowds continued to get larger and larger, and the protests reached a climax during one of the largest mass demonstrations in American history. On August 28, 1963—a warm summer's day—more than 200,000 blacks and whites marched arm in arm against racial injustice in what was billed as the March on Washington for Jobs and Freedom.

As the protesters marched from the Washington Monument to the Lincoln Memorial, they chanted the songs of the civil rights movement, including "We Shall Overcome" and "We Shall Not Be Moved," as well as a new tune, "Blowin' in the Wind," by a young singer named Bob Dylan. As the demonstrators approached the Lincoln Memorial for the climax of the day's events, King leaned toward Jackson and said, "Mahalia, why don't you sing 'I Been 'Buked and I Been Scorned' for us?" It was an old spiritual that had been popularized the year before by one of Jackson's friends, entertainer Harry Belafonte, but it was not widely known to white listeners. When the time came, Jackson stepped to the microphone and looked at the huge assembly. She began softly:

> I been 'buked and I been scorned,
> I'm gonna tell my Lord,
> When I get home,
> Just how long you've been treating me
>   wrong.

"As I sang the words," Jackson said later, "I heard a great murmur come rolling back to me from the multitude below and I sensed I had reached out and touched a chord."

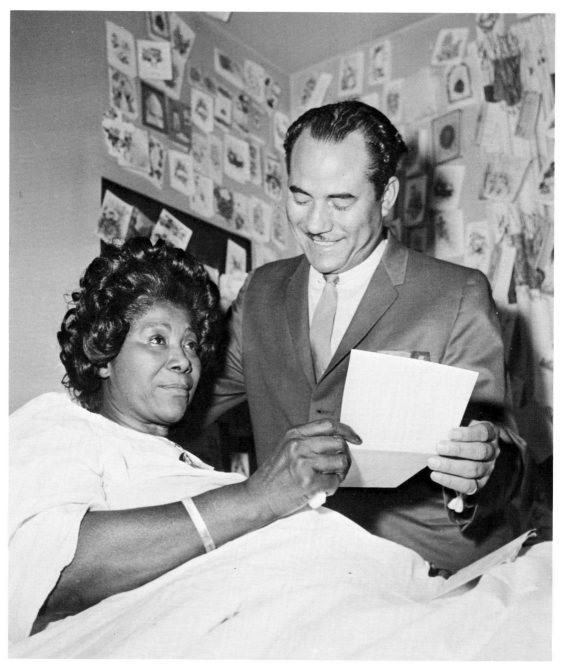

Jackson's second husband, Sigmund Galloway, joins his wife in her card-bedecked room during her 1964 hospitalization for a heart ailment.

Jackson (next to priest at lower right) listens as Martin Luther King, Jr., delivers his famous "I Have a Dream" speech at the March on Washington in 1963.

A few minutes later, Jackson sat down, and King got up to deliver the last speech of the day. His words would echo through history. "I have a dream," he cried, "that one day on the red hills of Georgia, the sons of former slaves and the sons of former slave owners will be able to sit down together at the table of brotherhood." The speech went on, building to an impassioned climax, and Jackson smiled when she recognized the quote that capped it off. It was from another old spiritual, which King often invoked to conclude his sermons:

Free at last!
Free at last!
Thank God Almighty,
We are free at last!

If Jackson ever had any doubts about whether her gospel music was being diluted by commercialism, or whether it was out of place in the modern world of jet planes and rock and roll, they were now dispelled for good. Her music did matter, and it was the heart and soul of a movement that was making monumental changes in the lives of her people.

Jackson sings with the Eureka Jazz Band during a return to her hometown of New Orleans in 1970. In the last years of her life she was regarded as one of America's most respected performers.

EIGHT

"I'm Going to Live the Life I Sing About"

For Mahalia Jackson—and everyone else involved in the civil rights movement during the summer of 1963—optimism abounded. But within a few short months, hope would be replaced by disillusionment. On November 22, 1963, President John F. Kennedy was assassinated in Dallas. In July 1964, the movement gained a major victory with the signing into law of the Civil Rights Act, which made all forms of racial discrimination illegal. Yet the legislation was unable to stem the tide of anger in the nation's black ghettos, and race riots exploded in the Watts section of Los Angeles that August. More riots followed, until by 1967 race riots had occurred in nearly every major American city.

In 1968 came the worst blow of all, when Martin Luther King, Jr., was struck down by an assassin's bullet in Memphis. The country was shocked by the killing of the man who had dedicated his life to racial equality and nonviolence. Renewed rage was the response in many inner cities, and rioting was still going on when King's body arrived for burial in Atlanta. At his funeral, which was televised throughout the stunned nation, an obviously shaken Jackson sang traditional spirituals in an unforgettably moving performance.

By this point, Jackson's health had become a serious problem. Her friend Studs Terkel recalled that "Mahalia had been ill, better, worse, better, worse" for most of the 1960s. The threat of recurring cancer was a constant worry, and her increasingly hectic schedule often drove her to the point of

Jackson and some neighborhood children advertise a benefit concert for the Mahalia Jackson Foundation. Problems with the nonprofit organization took their toll on Jackson's fragile health.

exhaustion. She suffered a series of heart attacks and lost almost 90 pounds. There were times, such as at a 1967 concert in New York's Philharmonic Hall, when her voice was so weak it barely rose above a whisper.

Jackson faced other personal problems as well. She had gone out with several men on a regular basis since her divorce from Ike Hockenhull in 1941, but none seriously enough for marriage. She wrote in her autobiography, "I used to joke with my Negro audiences at concerts and church meetings, 'Out of all the good-looking men I see here tonight I ought to be able to find myself a husband.' "

In 1964, Jackson began seeing Sigmund Galloway, a tall, soft-spoken building contractor from Gary, Indiana, whose family she had known for years. Galloway was also a musician—a flutist—and was playing in an orchestra in Los Angeles when Jackson began dating him regularly. Although Galloway was not really a gospel musician, he enjoyed working out modern arrangements of Jackson's old songs.

Jackson and her pianist, Edward Robinson, leave a West Berlin hospital in 1967; she became ill several times during her European tours.

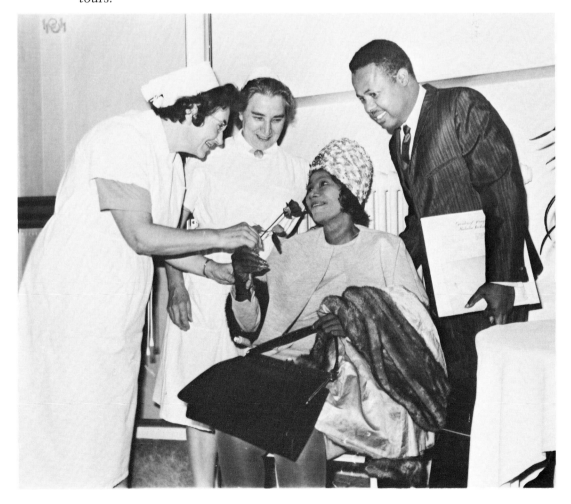

When he proposed to the 51-year-old Jackson in the spring of 1964, she accepted.

On the surface, it was an ideal marriage. National magazines published photographs of the happy couple looking at Jackson's scrapbooks. Galloway began appearing at Jackson's concerts, lining up musicians, playing the flute, sometimes even acting as master of ceremonies.

Beneath the surface, though, there were growing tensions. Galloway resented giving up his career and putting himself on Jackson's payroll. He also felt uneasy about being an interloper in an entourage that had been working with Jackson for many years. Moreover, he found himself living with a strong-willed woman who had been running her life by herself for more than two decades.

The marriage was short lived. In December 1966, Jackson and Galloway sued each other for divorce. (Ironically, Jackson's autobiography, *Movin' on Up*, written with magazine writer Evan Wylie, had been published just a few weeks before the divorce and was dedicated to Galloway.) The divorce case went to court and received a great deal of coverage in the press. When a decision was finally reached, the jury ruled in Jackson's favor, granting her a divorce on grounds of adultery and physical cruelty.

During the trial, *Jet*, one of the nation's leading black publications, revealed details of Jackson's finances and claimed she was an extremely wealthy woman. That revelation, when coupled with those that came out during the divorce proceedings, once again revived the issue of whether or not gospel singers should sing for money. By this point, Jackson was one of hundreds of professional gospel singers in America. Nevertheless, she felt the need to defend herself again and again. She continued to sing one of her favorites, "I'm Going to Live the Life I Sing About in My Songs," a tune written by Thomas A. Dorsey back when the issue of commercialism and gospel music was just starting to surface. One of the verses went

Every day, everywhere,
On the busy thoroughfare,
Folks may watch me, so they swat me,
Say I'm foolin', but I don't care,
I can't sing one thing and then live another,
Be a saint by day and a devil undercover,
I've got to sing about the life I live
In my songs.

Jackson also continued to defend her refusal to sing blues songs. "People were always pestering me to be a blues singer," she told a reporter around this time. "They'd tell me, 'Girl, you could be a blues singer.' I'd answer, 'What Negro couldn't be a blues singer?' I knew that wasn't the life for me. Blues are songs of despair."

In her later years, Jackson finally agreed to record a handful of nongospel songs, but none of them were blues. They were folk songs, like "Danny Boy" and "The Green Leaves of Summer," and Broadway show tunes, like "Sunrise, Sunset" and "Lost in the

Jackson at the climax of a West Berlin concert in the 1960s. She drew wildly enthusiastic audiences in Europe as fans on that continent embraced black music.

Stars." Nor did they become hits. The songs that became popular in her later years were pieces like "He's Got the Whole World in His Hands" and "I Can Put My Faith in Jesus." A few critics noted that Jackson's producers at Columbia were moving her away from the classic Chicago gospel of Thomas A. Dorsey and Roberta Martin. Instead, she was recording stereotypical spirituals, such as "Down By the Riverside" and "When the Saints Go Marching In." Yet Jackson still managed to get several "hard-edged" gospel songs into most of her albums.

As Jackson recorded more and more with lush orchestras and big choirs, she began to lose a segment of her black audience. But in their place was a new group of listeners who were white and middle class. At last, Jackson had achieved her long-held dream of gaining widespread popularity among whites. Yet it pained her to think that in doing so she had lost many of her black listeners.

During these years, younger performers often came to Jackson to ask her advice or to pay homage. She once told a group of aspiring singers, "I am famous through being disappointed. Accept your disappointments, let them make you wise and help you work. There is plenty of room at the top. New singers come up like fine grass. But you must study your music."

Jackson was fully aware of the number of singers, such as Sam Cooke, Little Richard, and Ray Charles, who used their gospel techniques to help forge soul and rock and roll, both of

Jackson sings at a memorial service for her friend Martin Luther King, Jr. The civil rights leader was assassinated in 1968.

which swept the nation in the late 1950s and early 1960s. The vocalist Aretha Franklin, who signed with Columbia in 1960 and soon became the leading young star of soul music, said that Jackson was her single most important influence. And in 1968, when Jackson first met rock-and-roll idol Elvis Presley in Hollywood, he rushed over to greet her, then moved his chair next to hers and took her hand as he told her that he had snuck into one of her church concerts in Mississippi when he was a teenager. "Mahalia," he finally said, "you're just like my mama."

Much of Jackson's energy in her later years was devoted to setting up the Mahalia Jackson Foundation, which for some time could only supply enough money for a modest scholarship at Roosevelt University in downtown Chicago. She tried hard to expand the foundation into something more ambitious, but it was a difficult process. Even her efforts to buy a site for the foundation headquarters proved to be tremendously frustrating.

Jackson spent a fair amount of her time on tour—especially in Europe, where her fans idolized her even more than they did in America—but there,

too, she was thwarted. She collapsed while in West Berlin in 1967 and had to cancel the tour and return home—a repeat of what happened to her in 1952. Yet she proved as resilient as ever. A 57-year-old Jackson surprised the audience at the 1970 Newport Jazz Festival by dancing a little as she sang "Just a Closer Walk with Thee." She sang with such intensity that her friends worried about the possibility of her collapsing again onstage. "I'm a mood singer," she reminded them. "I sing by feeling." Her life became even more upbeat when she and Sigmund Galloway remarried.

In April 1971, Jackson made a trip to Japan, where she sang before Emperor Hirohito on his 70th birthday. Then she continued on to India, where she

India's prime minister, Indira Gandhi, shakes hands with Jackson during Jackson's 1971 tour of Asia.

A proud Jackson displays an award she received from Chicago's De Paul University in 1971, when the school honored her for "serving God through the needs of men."

met Prime Minister Indira Gandhi. Photographers from the government-run United States Information Service followed her, confirming her status as an unofficial ambassador of goodwill. Upon her return to America, she appeared that fall on "The Flip Wilson Show," the first network television variety program starring a black comedian, and showed herself to be in fine form.

But when Jackson arrived in Europe to begin another tour that October, she fell ill once again and was flown home on a U.S. Army medical evacuation plane. After a brief stay in a hospital, she rallied, as she had done so many times before. With renewed effort, she set out to find a suitable site for her foundation headquarters. But the stress of the negotiations apparently caused a flare-up of an old heart problem. Whatever the reason, her health worsened, and early on the morning of January 27, 1972, at the Little Company of Mary Hospital in Chicago, Mahalia Jackson died. She was 59 years old.

Her body was taken back to the Greater Salem Baptist Church, where her aunt had first taken her 45 years before, when she first came to Chicago, and where she had begun her singing career with the Johnson Gospel Singers. All day long, friends and fans filed past her coffin to pay their respects—40,000 of them by final count. More than 6,000 people jammed into the large hall at the McCormick Place convention center for the funeral rites. Coretta Scott King, the widow of Martin Luther

Aretha Franklin sings a hymn at Mahalia Jackson's funeral in Chicago. Jackson died on January 27, 1972, at the age of 59.

A portrait of Jackson late in her life. A final tribute was paid Jackson by the people of New Orleans, 10,000 of whom filed by her casket prior to her burial in her old hometown.

King, Jr., addressed the mourners during the service, and entertainer Sammy Davis, Jr., read a telegram from President Richard Nixon. At the end of the speeches, Aretha Franklin sang Thomas A. Dorsey's best-known song, "Precious Lord, Take My Hand."

As the mourners filed out of the hall, many of them talked about Jackson's long career, of the various songs she had performed, of the concerts she had given, of the stories she had told. It seemed to these people that an era of American music had passed and that something irreplaceable had been lost. And, indeed, it had. "There are no more Mahalias," Jackson had told a group of young singers in 1967. "I am the last, and my success is the work of the Lord."

SELECTED DISCOGRAPHY

"The Queen of Gospel Singers," Mahalia Jackson often displayed tremendous versatility as a singer. The following albums should serve as a good introduction to her music.

Bless This House (Columbia PC 8761). Some of the best of Jackson's classic Columbia recordings, most of them dating from 1956. Includes her best-known version of "Summertime," which interpolates "Motherless Child"; Thomas A. Dorsey's classic "Take My Hand Precious Lord"; a stirring version of "The Lord's Prayer"; older gospel favorites such as "Let the Church Roll On"; and spirituals such as "Down by the Riverside."

Christmas with Mahalia (Columbia CS 9727). Familiar carols framed by elaborate orchestral arrangements; one of Jackson's last albums. Does not include her hit "Silent Night" but does offer a unique version of "What Child Is This," as well as "Silver Bells" and "White Christmas."

Greatest Hits (Columbia-Priority PC 37710). Not the original hits, but mostly re-creations recorded in Los Angeles in 1963. Versions of "In the Upper Room," "It Is No Secret (What God Can Do)," "How I Got Over," "Just Over the Hill," "Move On Up a Little Higher," and "Nobody Knows the Trouble I've Seen."

Mahalia Jackson Sings America's Favorite Hymns (Columbia CG 30744). Though not all of these songs are hymns, they include some of Jackson's best-known songs, such as "Didn't It Rain," "He's Got the Whole World in His Hands," "Jesus Met the Woman at the Well," "Go Tell It on the Mountain," "It Don't Cost Very Much," and "Walk All Over God's Heaven."

Mahalia Sings Best-Beloved Hymns of Dr. Martin Luther King (Columbia PC 9686). Includes liner notes by Coretta Scott King as well as songs such as "We Shall Overcome," "There Is a Balm in Gilead," "Evening Prayer," "Old Rugged Cross," "Rock of Ages," and "If I Can Help Somebody."

Twenty-one Greatest Hits (Kenwood 20510). An excellent collection of the best of the original Apollo recordings, first issued on 78-rpm singles from 1946–54. Many fans consider these sides to be Jackson's best work. Includes the original versions of many of the titles on *Greatest Hits,* as well as "His Eye Is on the Sparrow," "These Are They," "Silent Night," "Prayer Changes Things," and "The Last Mile of the Way."

CHRONOLOGY

Oct. 26, 1912	Born Mahala Jackson in New Orleans, Louisiana
1918	Mother, Charity, dies; Jackson moves in with Aunt Duke
1925	Jackson hears first blues records
1927	Moves to Chicago, Illinois
1928	Begins singing as a soloist; meets gospel composer Thomas A. Dorsey
1929	Joins Johnson Gospel Singers
1934	Takes eight-year-old John Sellers into her home
1936	Marries Ike Hockenhull
1937	Jackson makes first commercial recordings; changes first name to Mahalia
1939	Demonstrates gospel songs for Thomas A. Dorsey; opens beauty salon
1941	Divorces Hockenhull
1946	Signs recording contract with Apollo Records
1947	Recording of "Move on Up a Little Higher" becomes an immediate hit; Jackson hires pianist Mildred Falls as a full-time accompanist
1950	Conducts a seminar for jazz scholars at the Institute of Jazz Studies; gives first concert at Carnegie Hall
1952	Tours Europe: undergoes surgery for removal of a cancerous tumor
1954	Begins a series of radio shows for CBS; signs a recording contract with Columbia Records
1956	Sings at Democratic National Convention; befriends Martin Luther King, Jr., and becomes involved in the civil rights movement
1960	Performs at John F. Kennedy's presidential inauguration celebration
1963	Performs at the massive March on Washington for Jobs and Freedom
1965	Marries Sigmund Galloway
1966	Autobiography, *Movin' on Up*, is published; Jackson divorces Galloway
1970	Makes a comeback at the Newport Jazz Festival; remarries Galloway
Jan. 27, 1972	Mahalia Jackson dies in Chicago

FURTHER READING

Cornell, Jean Guy. *Mahalia Jackson, Queen of Gospel Song.* Champaign, IL: Garrard, 1974.

Goreau, Laurraine. *Just Mahalia, Baby.* Waco, TX: Word Books, 1975.

Hayes, Cedric J. *A Discography of Gospel Records 1937–1971.* Denmark: Karl Emil Knudsen, 1973.

Heilbut, Anthony. *The Gospel Sound: Good News and Bad Times.* Rev. ed. New York: Limelight Editions, 1985.

Jackson, Jesse. *Make a Joyful Noise Unto the Lord: The Life of Mahalia Jackson, Queen of Gospel Singers.* New York: Crowell, 1974.

Jackson, Mahalia, with Evan McLeod Wylie. *Movin' on Up.* New York: Hawthorn, 1966.

Lovell, John, Jr. *Black Song: The Forge and the Flame.* New York: Paragon House, 1986.

Reagon, Bernice Johnson, and Linn Shapiro, eds. *Roberta Martin and the Roberta Martin Singers: The Legacy and the Music.* Washington, D.C.: Smithsonian Institution, 1982.

Southern, Eileen. *The Music of Black Americans: A History.* New York: Norton, 1983.

INDEX

P I C T U R E   C R E D I T S

Charles K. Wolfe is a professor of English at Middle Tennessee State University near Nashville. He has authored or coauthored six books on American folk and popular music, including *Tennessee Strings, Kentucky Country*, and *Grand Ole Opry*. He has also written more than a hundred articles, published in such collections as *American Music* magazine, *The Encyclopedia of Southern Culture*, *The Journal of American Folklore*, and *The New Grove Dictionary of American Music*. A three-time Grammy nominee for his album liner notes, he has also worked as a producer and annotator for numerous record companies.

In addition, he writes a weekly column on gospel and folk music for the Brooklyn Academy of Music's newsletter on American music.

Charles Wolfe lives in Murfreesboro, Tennessee, with his wife and two daughters.

Matina S. Horner is president emerita of Radcliffe College and associate professor of psychology and social relations at Harvard University. She is best known for her studies of women's motivation, achievement, and personality development. Dr. Horner serves on several national boards and advisory councils, including those of the National Science Foundation, Time Inc., and the Women's Research and Education Institute. She earned her B.A. from Bryn Mawr College and Ph.D. from the University of Michigan, and holds honorary degrees from many colleges and universities, including Mount Holyoke, Smith, Tufts, and the University of Pennsylvania.